IDENTITIES AND AUDIENCES IN
THE MUSICAL

Identities and Audiences in the Musical

An Oxford Handbook of the American Musical, Volume 3

EDITED BY RAYMOND KNAPP

MITCHELL MORRIS

AND STACY WOLF

OXFORD
UNIVERSITY PRESS .

OXFORD
UNIVERSITY PRESS

Oxford University Press is a department of the University of Oxford. It furthers
the University's objective of excellence in research, scholarship, and education
by publishing worldwide. Oxford is a registered trade mark of Oxford University
Press in the UK and certain other countries.

Published in the United States of America by Oxford University Press
198 Madison Avenue, New York, NY 10016, United States of America.

© Oxford University Press 2018

Library of Congress Cataloging-in-Publication Data
Names: Knapp, Raymond. | Morris, Mitchell, 1961– | Wolf, Stacy Ellen.
Title: Identities and audiences in the musical : an Oxford handbook of the
American musical, Volume 3 / edited by Raymond Knapp,
Mitchell Morris, and Stacy Wolf.
Description: New York, NY : Oxford University Press, 2018. |
Series: Oxford handbooks | Includes bibliographical references and index.
Identifiers: LCCN 2018022283 | ISBN 9780190877798 (pbk. : alk. paper) |
ISBN 9780190877811 (epub)
Subjects: LCSH: Musicals—United States—History and criticism. | Fans (Persons)
Classification: LCC ML1711.I34 2018 | DDC 782.1/40973—dc23
LC record available at https://lccn.loc.gov/2018022283

1 3 5 7 9 8 6 4 2

Printed by WebCom, Inc., Canada

CONTENTS

CONTRIBUTORS

Steven Adler, Professor Emeritus of Theatre and Provost Emeritus of Earl Warren College, University of California, San Diego

Chase A. Bringardner, Associate Professor and Chair of Theatre, Auburn University

Jennifer Chapman, Associate Professor of Theatre Arts, University of Wisconsin-Eau Claire

Todd Decker, Professor and Chair of Music, Washington University in St. Louis

Michelle Dvoskin, Associate Professor of Theatre and Dance, Western Kentucky University

Raymond Knapp, Distinguished Professor of Musicology and Humanities, Academic Associate Dean of the Herb Alpert School of Music, and Director of the Center for Musical Humanities, University of California, Los Angeles

Mitchell Morris, Professor of Musicology and Humanities, University of California, Los Angeles

Holley Replogle-Wong, Lecturer in Musicology and Program Director of the Center for Musical Humanities, University of California, Los Angeles

David Savran, Distinguished Professor of Theatre and Vera Mowry Roberts Chair in American Theatre, the Graduate Center, City University of New York

Stacy Wolf, Professor of Theater and Director of the Program in Music Theater, Princeton University

ABOUT THE COMPANION WEBSITE

www.oup.com/us/iaaitm

Oxford has created a website to accompany *Identities and Audiences in the Musical*, which includes nearly two hundred audio, video, image, or text examples to illustrate or augment the discussions advanced in the text. To make this valuable resource easy to use, each example is keyed to its appropriate place in the text, and numbered sequentially within each of the essays that use this resource. For clarity, we've used the following notation (these particular indications would refer to examples 5-8 in the first essay):

🔊 Example 1.5 (Audio Example 1.5)

▶ Example 1.6 (Video Example 1.6)

🖼 Example 1.7 (Image Example 1.7)

📄 Example 1.8 (Text Example 1.8)

To access an example, simply click on the appropriate icon on the website.

IDENTITIES AND AUDIENCES IN THE MUSICAL

Introduction

THE AMERICAN MUSICAL IS A paradox. On stage or screen, musicals at once hold a dominant and a contested place in the worlds of entertainment, art, and scholarship. Born from a mélange of performance forms that included opera and operetta, vaudeville and burlesque, minstrelsy and jazz, musicals have always sought to amuse more than instruct, and to make money more than make political change. In spite of their unapologetic commercialism, though, musicals have achieved supreme artistry and have influenced culture as much as if not more than any other art form in America, including avantgarde and high art on the one hand, and the full range of popular and commercial art on the other. Reflecting, refracting, and shaping U.S. culture since the early twentieth century, musicals converse with shifting dynamics of gender and sexuality, ethnicity and race, and the very question of what it means to be American and to be human. The musical explores identity, self-determination, and the American dream.

The form of the musical—the combination of music, dance, speech, and design—is paradoxical, too. By the middle of the twentieth century, spoken scenes in musicals were expected to conform to the style of nonmusical plays, with characters psychologized and realistically portrayed. When characters burst into song or dance, a different expressive mode took over, one that scholars like Richard Dyer have seen as utopian.[1] Even as artists aimed for "integration" among the musical's disparate parts, in emulation of Wagner's "total artwork," the pieces required different skills of creation, presentation, and interpretation. As Scott McMillin argues in *The Musical as Drama*, "When a musical is working well, I feel the crackle of difference...between the book and the numbers, between songs and dances, between dance and spoken dialogue."[2] In part because of its hybrid form and its commercial aspirations, the musical failed to register as a legitimate topic for scholarly study in either music or theater programs in universities until near the end of the twentieth century. Although audiences flocked to see *The Phantom of the Opera* on Broadway to the tune of 140 million people (as of 2017) worldwide since its opening year on Broadway (1987), and the film of *The Sound of Music* (1965) held its place as the most popular movie musical of all time well into the twenty-first century, few college courses taught the history or criticism of musicals. And while young composers, lyricists, librettists, designers, and performers honed their craft and enrolled in professional training programs, they gained knowledge of the musical's history and theory through practice rather than through college classes that emphasized a scholarly approach to musicals.

Beginning in the 1990s, and gaining considerable momentum across the first decade(s) of the new millennium, the study of American musicals on stage and on film has grown rapidly into a legitimate field. Many universities now offer surveys of musical theater or film history; or build a course focused on a composer, a subgenre, or a period in U.S. history; or include musicals in other courses, from American drama to popular culture to African American studies.[3] In departments of music and musicology, theater, film, media studies, and literature, more courses are taught each year about musicals or include the study of a musical play or film as an example of cultural or performance history. Increasingly, musical theater, musical films, and musicals in other media, such as television or online, are seen as viable objects of scholarly inquiry.

Scholarship to support the study of musicals is gradually catching up to the enthusiastic reception of students, as more dissertations are written and books published on musicals each year. Where there were formerly only encyclopedic lists of musicals and their creators, coffee-table tomes, or hagiographies, there is now a growing field of academic studies of musicals. Some explicate and analyze a range of musicals; others trace a chronological history. Some authors stress context over analysis, locating musicals historically, and some books consider musicals from specific identity positions. Increasingly, studies focus on a single musical, often relying on archival research to unearth details about the production process. Finally, books take a biographical approach and center on a director, composer, choreographer, producer, performer, or another member of the creative team.

Even as scholarship has grown in diverse and wide-ranging ways, the teaching of musicals continues to be extremely challenging. This book, in its original one-volume edition, grew out of our mutual passion for teaching musicals and our mutual frustration with available pedagogically oriented materials. When the three of us first met to talk about musicals, we complained—as most professors do—about the lack of a textbook for teaching musicals that adequately covered the wide range of possible approaches to the subject. Each of us had solved the problem in our own way, using a combination of texts and articles and our own expertise. From that start, we found common goals as instructors: first, to situate the musical historically; second, to locate the ideological work of the musical as "American"; and third, to practice a variety of methods and techniques to analyze musicals. Moreover, each of us was well aware of the strengths and weaknesses in our training, of the stubborn disciplinarity of each of our fields, and of the tendency to privilege one element of the musical over another based on our comfort level. We knew that a useful textbook for the study of the American musical needed more than our three voices to write it.

Although we designed our book as a teaching tool, we mean "teaching" in the broadest possible way for students, instructors, and the general reader. We intended our book not (necessarily) to be read cover to cover, nor (necessarily) assigned in order, but as a resource for instructors, students, and aficionados of the musical and as a complement to other studies currently available. As well, scholars expert in one area of the musical might use our book as a first resource in coming to terms with other aspects of the art form less familiar to them and as an additional resource for courses on related topics, such as Tin Pan Alley or Popular Song.

Since the publication of *The Oxford Handbook of the American Musical* in 2011, the American musical continues to thrive, both reflecting and shaping cultural values and social norms, and even commenting on politics, whether directly and on a national scale (*Hamilton* [2015]) or somewhat more obliquely and on a more intimate scale (*Fun Home* [2015]). New stage musicals, such as *Come from Away* (2017) and *The Band's Visit* (2017), open on Broadway every season, challenging conventions of form and content, and revivals offer audiences a different perspective on extant shows (*Carousel* [2018]; *My Fair Lady* [2018]). Television musicals broadcast live, including *Peter Pan Live!* (2014) and *The Wiz Live!* (2015), at once hearken back to 1950s television's affection for musical theatre and aim to attract new audiences through the accessibility of television. Film musicals, including *Les Misérables* (2012) and *Into the Woods* (2014), capitalize on the medium's technical capabilities of perspective and point of view, as well as visual spectacle. Television has embraced the genre anew, and with unexpected gusto, not only devising musical episodes for countless dramatic and comedy series, but also generating musical series such as *Galavant* (2015-16) and *Crazy Ex-Girlfriend* (2015-).

And animated musicals, such as Disney's *Moana* (2016), hail child and adult audiences with their dual messages, vibrant visual vocabulary, and hummable music.

The essays gathered in this book, Volume III of the reissued *Oxford Handbook,* are written by leading scholars in the field, and explore the American musical from both the outside and the inside. The first half collects articles that analyze how musicals have addressed important issues of identity in American culture. The second half moves outside the musicals themselves to consider aspects of their sustaining receptive environment.

Issues of identity, regarding both representation and embodiment, have always been central to the American musical in all its guises. Who appears in musicals, who (or what) they are meant to represent, and how, over time, those representations have been understood and interpreted, provide the very basis for our engagement with the genre. The essays gathered in the first half of this book each focus on a separate dimension of identity, beginning with two groupings that have received a great deal of attention—race and ethnicity, and gender and sexuality—due to both the contested nature and history of those identities in American culture, and to the musical's capacity to bring those identities to the fore in myriad ways. The third chapter of this section explores somewhat less traveled ground, considering how regional identity has played out against national identity in some musicals, whereas the final chapter considers how the genre itself, with its vexed history of undervaluation, entails crucial issues of class and cultural standing.

As important as the question of who appears in musicals are the questions of who watches and listens to them, and of how specific cultures of reception attend differently to the musical, affecting how the American musical has mattered to a variety of audiences across its history. Basic to these considerations are the ever-shifting financial constraints that govern how musicals get to be made in the first place, a perspective that understands audiences as, first of all, paying customers; box office is thus the central concern of the first chapter in this section. The following two chapters take up issues of reception from different perspectives, first from that of actual audiences and influential critics, then from that of the sustaining culture of fandom, crucial for understanding both the continued vitality of the genre and its persistently low cultural standing. The final two chapters then take up two central aspects of the genre as a way to return attention to the genre's actual constitution: its enduring performance traditions in regional, community, and school theater programs, and its "reflexive idealism," which both invests it with meanings vital to its audiences and renders its aspirational dimension suspect to the guardians of high culture.

Owing both to the musical's engagement with identity and embodiment on all levels, and to its commercial setting and intimate engagements with audiences, it is perhaps the most intricately collaborative art and entertainment form in US culture. When audiences experience the emotional tug and infectious energy of a musical, they form bonds of identification and enhanced empathy across a spectrum of group identities, and take those bonds into their lives, whether attitudinally, or by reenacting them both through private and internalized performance. Through fandom and local theatrical traditions, they partake even of the collaborative (and fiscal) dimensions of musicals, learning, like their professional counterparts, to participate in art-making with others, the better to connect, if only as fans, with what the great composer and lyricist Stephen Sondheim told *Hamilton* creator Lin-Manuel Miranda: "Well, I collaborate with people. My spark often comes from collaborators. . . . I mean, I'm a collaborative animal. . . . I need the spur. And the spur and the boost comes [*sic*] from somebody else, generally."[4]

Raymond Knapp

ACKNOWLEDGMENTS

Any book this complex—like the musical itself—has innumerable contributors beyond those headlined as editors and authors. The editors are extremely grateful for the abundant and varied support their scholarly communities have provided. On the institutional level, this included support, at UCLA, from the Office of Instructional Development, the Department of Musicology, and the Council on Research, along with a rich field of interactions among students and other faculty; we are especially grateful for insights that have found their way into this book from Juliana Gondek, Peter Kazaras, Elijah Wald, Sam Baltimore, Sarah Ellis, and Holley Replogle-Wong, and for Holley's exemplary work preparing and organizing materials for the book's Web site. At Princeton, we thank the Lewis Center for the Arts, especially Chair Michael Cadden. We thank Senior Production Editor Joellyn Ausanka for guiding us through the copyediting and proofing stages of the book. Norm Hirschy at Oxford University Press has been unfailingly, even brilliantly helpful, at every step of the process. And, for the reissued volumes, we have been blessed with the guidance, expertise, and patience of Lauralee Yeary.

Raymond Knapp, Mitchell Morris, Stacy Wolf

NOTES

1. Richard Dyer, "Entertainment and Utopia," in *Genre: The Musical*, ed. Rick Altman (London: Routledge and Kegan Paul, 1981); originally published in *Movie* 2 [Spring 1977]: 2–13).
2. Scott McMillin, *The Musical as Drama: A Study of the Principles and Conventions behind Musical Shows from Kern to Sondheim* (Princeton: Princeton University Press, 2006), p. 2.
3. See Stacy Wolf, "In Defense of Pleasure: Musical Theatre History in the Liberal Arts [A Manifesto]," *Theatre Topics* 17.1 (March 2007): 51–60.

4. Lin-Manuel Miranda, "Stephen Sondheim, Theater's Greatest Lyricist," *New York Times*, October 16, 2017. https://www.nytimes.com/2017/10/16/t-magazine/lin-manuel-miranda-stephen-sondheim.html?_r=0 Accessed November 25, 2017.

PART ONE

IDENTITIES

1

Race, Ethnicity, Performance

TODD DECKER

■ □ ■

*We deplore the evil of stereotypes in fiction, on the stage and on the
screen—the crap-shooting, razor wielding Negro, the crafty and pe-
nurious Jew, the pugnacious, whiskey drinking Irishman. All these
are on their way out as stock characters. When races are invariably
symbolized by these types, the result is not only harmful but it is
likely to make dull entertainment.*[1]

OSCAR HAMMERSTEIN II WROTE THIS assessment in 1948,
and in one sense he was right: negative theatrical stereotypes
were on the way out in the immediate postwar years. Whether
these stereotypes made for "dull entertainment" is debatable.
Aimed at specific audiences, the stereotypes Hammerstein
listed had been highly successful, and in their day they were
the very antithesis of "dull entertainment." Throughout its
history, the musical has relied on the dramaturgical short-
hand stereotypes provide, chiefly as a means to enhance the
entertainment value of a product being sold to particular
audiences.

Hammerstein's short list of hateful stereotypes—the kind
any enlightened person would see as wrong—fails to include
others carrying more ambiguous meanings: the exaggerated
smiles and good spirits of black mammy figures, "hot-blooded"
Latin types, "wise" Asians, laconic Native Americans, "lazy"
black males who avoid work by moving and talking slowly

(exemplified by the African American actor Stepin Fetchit, a major Hollywood star in the 1930s), stuffy Germans, and accent-based characters from anywhere whose humorously incorrect use of a second language provokes laughter in an audience of native speakers.

Hammerstein's negative types and the more ambiguous "comic" types listed above together form an array of racial and ethnic masks familiar throughout popular culture history, including the musical. These combinations of costume, makeup, posture, accent, character traits, and narrative possibilities have gone in and out of fashion and acceptability. Some provided an excuse for exotic or spectacular display. Others offered cover for social or political satire. All are the products of particular social and historical circumstances. When circumstances change, typically, stereotypes do as well. Deeply embedded in the ever-changing social fabric of the nation, ethnic and racial stereotypes are frequently the most dated aspects of musical shows and films for later audiences, and while they can be softened or excised completely in later productions on stage, they live forever in films.

In musical terms, racial and ethnic masks might take the form of a melody that sounds foreign, such as the pentatonic "Oriental" sound of Richard Rodgers's "March of the Siamese Children" from *The King and I*, or complex rhythms suggesting a particular geographic origin, such as the "Latin" cross rhythms in Leonard Bernstein's "America" from *West Side Story*. These harmonic or rhythmic tropes assume a racially unmarked musical style to which the exotic effects are added. In similar fashion, racial and ethnic stereotypes are most often added to a show or film otherwise populated by ethnically and racially unmarked "white" characters with whom the broadest audience in a majority white nation can identify. Audiences for the Broadway and Hollywood musical have been consistently urban, middle and upper class, and white. It's no surprise that ethnic and racial others usually turn up as comic sidekicks rather than romantic leads or figures of authority.

The racial and ethnic masks prominent in the history of the musical are double-edged. Some have distorted particular groups in pernicious ways, causing lingering cultural effects as undeniable as they are immeasurable. Others did significant work helping select groups assimilate, facilitating passage into the unmarked collective called white. Andrea Most, among others, has argued that in the case of Jewish Americans, the opportunity to put on and take off a comic Jewish mask, among others in their repertoire, served performers such as Eddie Cantor well, allowing them to argue for the full inclusion of Jews as assimilated, racially unmarked Americans.[2]

Because the musical thrives on exaggeration, the ethnic and racial masks deployed throughout its history have represented racial and ethnic others in an altogether unsubtle fashion. This license to exaggerate is inevitably expanded if the audience has no real knowledge of the group being represented. Such is the case with blackface, easily the most influential mask in the history of the musical. For example, Sophie Tucker broke through on the vaudeville circuit in the 1900s by appearing as a blackface coon shouter. At the turn of the twentieth century, coon songs and shouters presented some of the harshest, most baldly racist stereotypes ever to appear in popular music. They were tremendously popular with audiences in northern cities that were experiencing an explosion in their African American populations as rural southern blacks migrated north, seeking greater opportunities and less racism. At the end of her coon-shouting act, Tucker would remove a single glove, revealing to the audience that she was, in fact, white. In her autobiography, Tucker reports that cries of amazement from her audiences followed the revelation of her actual racial identity.[3] That northern audiences could have mistaken Tucker for a black performer indicates that the derogatory stereotypes of blackface coon shouters were doing powerful cultural work. As Tucker's example shows, control over racial or ethnic masks is central to a performer's power over her career.

Pulling off a glove and provoking the audience's wonder at an act of racial mimicry—however false the stereotype—has not been an option for African American performers, who labor under a different set of assumptions in a nation historically obsessed with segregating black from white in all areas, including the musical. African Americans on the musical stage and screen have more often than not found their careers fundamentally shaped by their skin color. Their perceived black identity prevents African American performers from freely taking up or setting down ethnic and racial masks. This is not to say that performers with visibly Latin or Asian identities have not been similarly limited. In terms of musical style, however, Latin-inspired music has not affected the sound of the musical beyond its use as an exotic "tinge," and Asian-derived sounds have had little to no presence outside of "oriental" tropes drawn from European classical music and American popular song. Yet, as with virtually every kind of twentieth-century American popular music, the musical stage and screen has been intimately linked to African American musical styles; moreover, African Americans as a group have played defining roles as performers on the musical stage (as the long history of black-cast shows attests).

The distinction between black and white—a matter of perceived racial identity, of literally judging performers by their skin color—has had a structuring role across the history of the musical. This color line inevitably defines the history of the musical even as it defines the history of the nation. Often, but not always, the color line comes into focus when we attend closely to when and how black musical style and African American performers have been brought into the musical, a genre that has remained chiefly concerned with celebrating a functioning national community understood almost always to be, like the musical's primary audience, white.[4] To illustrate the central importance of race in American musicals, and especially the black/white color line, I focus for the remainder of this chapter on a series of case studies—selected stage and screen musicals and performers from the 1920s, 1940s, and 1950s—before concluding with a consideration of 1990s revivals.[5]

NARRATIVE AND MUSICAL STYLE IN THE 1920S

The Broadway stage was at its peak in production activity and cultural power during the 1920s, a period when African American performers and musical style had a tremendous impact on the musical. The 1920s were ushered in by the first black-cast hit of the Jazz Age: *Shuffle Along* opened in 1921 and played 484 performances (placing it among the longest-running shows of the decade). Unlike most black-cast shows then and after, *Shuffle Along* not only starred African Americans but was written and produced by African Americans as well. In a score dominated by high-energy rhythm numbers, composer Eubie Blake and lyricist Noble Sissle took a risk with the song "Love Will Find a Way." This love duet for the romantic leads is unmarked by tropes of blackness and would easily fit into any operetta of the time. With a broad melody and senti-mental lyrics in standard, rather flowery English, "Love Will Find a Way" characterized *Shuffle Along*'s black lovers as just like any other lovers—meaning white lovers—on the musical stage (◐ Example 1.1). Sissle and Blake feared there might be a negative response from a Broadway audience unused to black characters presented in non-stereotypical ways. Contrary to these fears, the song was greeted respectfully, although it didn't become a hit. (The 2016 musical *Shuffle Along, or the Making of the Musical Sensation of 1921 and All That Followed* recreated this concern while restaging "Love Will Find a Way," with performer Audra MacDonald playing the actress Lottie Gee telegraphing concern over audience reception of the love song while singing it in the dramatic context of the original *Shuffle Along*.) There have been few follow-ups to "Love Will Find a Way." For black performers, doing "white" musical numbers has never been as profitable as emphasizing the link between black performers and black musical styles.

The success of *Shuffle Along* led to a string of jazzy black-cast shows across the 1920s, which in turn created a sizable pool of experienced African American talent in New York. By the 1927–28 season, white producers were calling on black performers in unprecedented numbers. The only show still revived from this period is *Show Boat*, which opened in December 1927. Defying the pattern of segregating black and white performers from each other in different shows, *Show Boat* calls for an interracial cast of black and white performers (one of just a handful of such shows in Broadway history). With book and lyrics by Hammerstein and music by Jerome Kern, *Show Boat* was structured around the visible and audible differences between its black and white cast members. Racial identity defines everyone in *Show Boat*, an exceptional work that interrogates the absurdities and tragedies of racism even as it inevitably reinforces the racial stereotypes of the period.

Based on Edna Ferber's best-selling novel of 1926, the story of *Show Boat* centers on a white couple—Gaylord Ravenal and Magnolia Hawkes—who meet and marry in the romantic context of a floating theater on the Mississippi River in the late nineteenth century. Ravenal, a gambler whose luck finally runs out, abandons Magnolia in Chicago, leaving her to support and raise their young daughter. In the novel, the couple never reconciles. But the musical demands happy endings, and in the stage version *Show Boat* ends with the lovers reunited on the boat where they first fell in love. A secondary plot involving Julie, a light-skinned black woman trying (unsuccessfully) to pass as white, is skillfully worked into Magnolia and Ravenal's story. When Ravenal abandons Magnolia, she is able to earn a living singing on the stage, drawing on her experience as a performer on the floating theater, where she had learned how to sing from Joe, a black worker on the showboat and a decidedly minor character in the novel. Kern and Hammerstein saw the potential to expand the part of Joe on the musical stage by building the character around Paul Robeson, a charismatic performer with undeniable star quality for New York's white audience. Robeson, who had appeared in plays and sung sold-out recitals of Negro spirituals, initially refused the role of Joe—he eventually played the part in London (1928), on Broadway (1932), and in a Hollywood film (1936)—but the song Kern and Hammerstein wrote for him, "Ol' Man River," found great success in the original stage production of *Show Boat* and after.[6]

While building *Show Boat* around the opportunity to feature Robeson in an operetta centered on a white romance, Kern, Hammerstein, and producer Florenz Ziegfeld expanded the black presence in the show, hiring an entire chorus of African American singers and dancers. There was no precedent in the novel for this decision. Numbering over forty, the black chorus performed a full range of '20s black musical theater types: serious spiritual-type numbers, high-spirited levee dances in modest southern costumes, jazzy dances in glitzy contemporary clothes, even an ironic "jungle" number as black New Yorkers hired to play African villagers for an anthropological exhibit at the 1893 Chicago World's Fair. The men of the black chorus opened the show singing "Niggers all work on de Mississippi/Niggers all work whil' de white folks play." This delineation of the color line was strong stuff then and proved unrevivable in later decades, when the opening words of both lines were replaced by "colored folks work," "darkies all work," and the racially neutral "here we all work."

Despite their being featured throughout the show, none of the black chorus's numbers connected directly to the story of the white lovers Magnolia and Gaylord: the black chorus added to the entertainment value of *Show Boat* but did not participate in the plot (except through Julie). In the subsequent revivals and film versions of *Show Boat*, of which there have been many, the story of the white lovers remained intact while many of the black chorus numbers so important to the 1927 original were cut, often because later audiences found these 1920s stereotypes to be unacceptably, irredeemably racist.[7]

The first commercially successful sound film with synchronized lip movements opened in 1927 just a few weeks before *Show Boat*. *The Jazz Singer* remains one of the most intensely Jewish films ever released for a general audience: it is also a story that celebrates Broadway as the pinnacle of American success. The central character, Jakie Rabinowitz, grows up in an orthodox Jewish home on Manhattan's Lower East Side. His rabbi father forbids him to sing jazz, which in this context means American popular music. But Jakie wants to go on the stage, and he runs away to be a performer, eventually earning the chance to appear in a big-time Broadway show. Returning to his parents' home for the first time as an adult, Jakie finds his father gravely ill and unable to sing for services on the most sacred night of the Jewish year—the very night Jakie's Broadway show is to open.

Al Jolson, a seasoned Broadway star who built his success performing both in and out of blackface, played the part of Jakie. In *The Jazz Singer*, nothing in Jolson's performance style is typed as black (in other contexts, he did play a stereotypical "darky," although always with his signature style). Indeed Jakie's Jewish heritage—his "tear in the voice"—is understood to be the source of his extraordinary ability to sell a song: the blackface mask is simply part of the Jolson persona. The conflict at the heart of *The Jazz Singer* is lodged within Jakie's character: will he be true to his faith and family and sing on the holiest day of the Jewish year or will he honor the American show business creed that dictates the show must go on? In the end, Jakie—and the film audience—has it both ways: the opening is postponed while Jakie sings the Kol Nidre in his dying father's place; in the next scene, Jakie's knockin' 'em dead on Broadway, singing a mammy song to his teary-eyed mother in the front row. In this one instance in *The Jazz Singer*, it may appear that Jolson matches the blackface mask with a racial stereotype: the mammy singer. But he sings completely without an accent and, as noted, addresses the song directly to his Jewish mother (🔊 Example 1.2). For a late 1920s audience, the mammy singer was less a black stereotype that represented some essential quality of African Americans than a Jolson routine, a show-biz pose associated with a specific star performer. Of course, Jolson's power over the blackface mask—his ability, like Tucker's, to put it on and take it off at will—should not be overlooked.

The pain and pleasure of assimilation explored in *The Jazz Singer* became an enduring part of the affirming American story told again and again by the musical. It could be translated into almost any ethnic other (see the discussion of *Flower Drum Song* later in the chapter.). But it would be impossible to make a version of *The Jazz Singer* where Jolson's character was black. The African American experience is fundamentally unlike that of immigrant groups who came on their own terms rather than through force. And while the assimilation story at the heart of *The Jazz Singer* seems made for the celebratory mode of the musical, the very different historical experience of African Americans is not so easy to render in the simplified narrative patterns of the musical.[8]

EXOTIC "OTHER" WOMEN
IN 1940S HOLLYWOOD

The contrasting careers of Carmen Miranda, the embodiment of a particular Latin stereotype, and Lena Horne, the only African American woman to sign a star contract with a major Hollywood studio, highlight how ethnicity and race played out during the glory years of the musical screen. Miranda and Horne attained Hollywood stardom at almost exactly the same time—Miranda in 1940, Horne in 1942—and their relatively brief careers ended around the same time as well. Both appeared in only one studio-era film after 1950. But the way Hollywood integrated Miranda and Horne into the world of the film musical was fundamentally different. While Miranda was able to bring an exaggerated ethnic color to both the music and the plot of the films she starred in—endearing her to the audience as an animated individual who spoke as well as sang—Horne's refined persona was confined to musical numbers only.

Carmen Miranda came to Hollywood from Brazil by way of Broadway. She appeared in fourteen films between 1940 and 1953, almost all in Technicolor, an expensive process suited to her signature lavish costumes and bright red lipstick. Miranda usually played a nightclub performer, which allowed her to offer several musical numbers and also take a supporting comic role in the plot. Most of her films provide ample space for Miranda's over-the-top persona as "the lady in the tutti-frutti hat." Miranda's musical numbers invariably involved the sights and sounds of an all-male Latin band: either the Bando da Lua, a group of light-skinned, middle-class Brazilians who traveled to New York with Miranda for her first Broadway appearances, or later, at MGM, Xavier Cugat's extremely popular band. Miranda was Brazilian (although born in Portugal) and Cugat, a classically trained violinist, was Spanish by way of Cuba: in the boiled-down logic of American popular music, they both made "Latin" music (Example 1.3). Hollywood made little attempt to distinguish between different national styles: South America was conceptualized as an undifferentiated cultural area, exuberantly colorful and filled with rhythms defined collectively as "Latin."

In her songs *con movimientos*, Miranda usually appeared surrounded by a group of men playing various Latin hand percussion instruments and guitars, dancing simple but (for that time) sexy steps, with lots of hip-swinging and leg-showing. Generic "Latin" rhythms packaged for a mass audience have periodically hit it big, and Miranda led the explosion of Latin-tinged music that coincided with the wartime Good Neighbor Policy, an effort to solidify U.S. ties with South America by cultural as well as political means. Miranda was often allowed a sexual role in her films as well, typically as an exotic figure of desire for older white male comic characters. In *The Gang's All Here* (1943), she manipulates Edward Everett Horton by covering his face with red kisses, marks indicative more of his desire than of any real danger posed by Miranda. Her playful, slightly naughty, in the end innocent and joyous sexuality was a key part of Miranda's attraction. However excessive and campy her persona might appear in retrospect, the films viewed whole tell a different story. Behind her malapropisms and frequent lapses into lightning-fast Portuguese lay a conniving mind that was frequently running the show.[9] She provided a capable ally to the white ingénue at the center of virtually all her films—a bit of wishful political allegory, perhaps—and even if she wasn't at the center of the plot, a Carmen Miranda film is typically filled with the Brazilian bombshell's defining presence from start to finish.

Lena Horne made her first big splash in the early 1940s at Café Society, a New York nightclub that allowed black and white patrons to sit together at a time when nightlife, like most of American society, was segregated. Wartime pressure on the film industry encouraged the studios to expand the possibilities for black performers, and Horne was the primary beneficiary of this push to change Hollywood's presentation of African Americans. In 1942, Horne signed a star contract with MGM, but once they had her, the studio didn't know what to do with her. The Production Code, an informal agreement among the studios defining acceptable film content, forbade any suggestion of romance between black and white characters or actors. Horne could not flirt with her white co-stars like Miranda could, and without African American peers to play opposite her, there was little means to insert Horne into the plot. She did star in two black-cast films—*Cabin in the Sky* and *Stormy Weather*, both 1943—but these proved to be historical anomalies.[10] And so, Horne appeared as herself in a series of minimally produced musical segments, inserted as specialty numbers unconnected to the plots of their films. An intensely photogenic subject, Horne typically sang one, sometimes two songs dressed in an elegant gown, usually standing almost entirely still. She always received a glamorizing close-up, treatment that created the aura of the star around her. But the limits on Horne's participation in these films were severe. Musically, Horne's subtle, rather personal style—shaped in the 1930s when she toured as a singer with both black and white bands—was ideal for the screen, and her solos, such as "Honeysuckle Rose" from *Thousands Cheer* (1943), remain highlights of the era (🔊 Example 1.4).[11] But since there was no possibility of tying Horne into the plots of her films, she languished as a specialty performer, boxed in by the realities of the movie business. Horne was deeply dissatisfied with the limitations Hollywood put on her talent, and after negotiating a contract that gave her most of the year free to perform elsewhere— highly exceptional for MGM—she asked to be released in 1950.

LIVING ROOMS AND NIGHTCLUBS IN FLOWER DRUM SONG (1958 AND 2002)

In the postwar decades, Hammerstein collaborated with composer Richard Rodgers on a series of musicals that brought Asians and Asian Americans into the Broadway musical in a substantial way for the first time. *South Pacific* (1949), *The King and I* (1951), and *Flower Drum Song* (1958) form a triptych of Asian-themed musicals that found commercial success. Only two similar shows have played Broadway in the seventy years since, neither scoring as hits: *Pacific Overtures* (1976, a meditation on Japanese history with music and lyrics by Stephen Sondheim) and *Allegiance* (2015, a story of Japanese Americans interned during World War II, based on the experiences of the show's star, George Takei).[12] Asian stereotypes—comic, serious, or otherwise—have never been staples of the American musical and there has never been a sizable group of Asian American musical theater professionals. Given the outsized influence of Hammerstein, the musical with Asian characters is a writer's rather than a performer's tradition. In this light, the original and revised versions of *Flower Drum Song* offer an illuminating comparison, especially as this is the only one of the five "Asian" musicals set in the contemporary United States and directly concerned with questions of assimilation. And just as *The Jazz Singer* centered on the irreconcilable distance between the synagogue and the Broadway stage, *Flower Drum Song* turns on the contrast between a traditional Chinese home and an American-style nightclub.

Adapted from a 1957 novel by Chinese immigrant C. Y. Yee, *Flower Drum Song* opened in 1958, and a widescreen color film version followed soon after in 1961. Set in contemporary San Francisco, *Flower Drum Song* tells a multigenerational tale of tradition and assimilation by the gentlest of means. Largely lacking in spectacle and set almost entirely in domestic spaces, *Flower Drum Song* is the most play-like of Rodgers and Hammerstein's musical plays. While the revival trend of the 1990s and 2000s saw the return to Broadway of many classic Rodgers and Hammerstein shows in slightly altered form, none were subjected to the comprehensive overhaul *Flower Drum Song* received. David Henry Hwang, the most successful Asian American playwright of his generation, worked with director/choreographer Robert Longbottom to create an entirely new plot, retaining only the songs from the original. As Hwang noted in his introduction to the printed libretto, "I don't think a single line remains from the original book." The original production was modestly successful (seventeen months on Broadway followed by seventeen months on national tour); the revisal, which opened on Broadway in 2002, was a commercial failure.

The original *Flower Drum Song* tells the story of Mei Li, a Chinese girl who comes to San Francisco for an arranged marriage with Sammy Fong, owner of a Chinatown nightclub. Sammy doesn't want to follow through on the marriage contract—his mother arranged the match—and he convinces the father of Wang Ta to accept Mei Li as an ideal traditional Chinese bride for his son. Ta describes himself early on as "both" Chinese and American, saying "sometimes the American half shocks the Oriental half." He wants to choose his own bride and already has someone in mind, a Chinese American girl named Linda Low who, unbeknownst to Ta, works as a dancer at Sammy's nightclub and is, in fact, Sammy's lover. After Ta sees the assimilated Linda doing a Chinese-themed striptease at Sammy's club, his interest turns definitively toward Mei Li, who maintains a slight accent and modest demeanor throughout. Mei Li's appearance at a party scene in a glamorous yet tasteful American dress visually argues for her potential to assimilate just the right amount for Ta's sense of himself as "both" Chinese and American. Ta's father and aunt, gently comic elders, are major characters and Ta's family home—"architecturally Victorian with Chinese decoration superimposed"—is the primary setting. Traditional ways preserved by Chinatown's elders and the modern American ways of the children are juxtaposed throughout. In the end, the couples are sorted out in satisfactory fashion—Ta with Mei Li, Sammy with Linda—by way of the word "wetback," a contemporary racial epithet for an illegal Mexican immigrant. Spoken by Mei Li at the crucial moment—she learns the word watching late night TV—"wetback" assumes comic proportions as the children manage to get their way with their parent's blessings to boot, a thoroughly American result.

Two-thirds of the way into act one, we find ourselves at the graduation celebration of the Marina American Citizenship School. The scene typifies the gentle approach Hammerstein's version takes to questions of ethnicity and assimilation. Madame Liang, played by Juanita Hall, says, "I am proud to be both Chinese and American" and compares living in America to "that Chinese dish that the Americans invented." (Hall, a light-skinned African American, had played the much less subtly drawn Bloody Mary in *South Pacific*.) Liang then leads the group in "Chop Suey," a catalog song about late 1950s American life that is largely unmarked by Chinese examples. One can imagine almost any group of older ethnic "others" singing the song, which expresses excitement about citizenship in a modern country (● Example 1.5). The only Chinese thing about the number is the title, which "Americans invented" after all. "Chop Suey" can be read as a reply to the more aggressive young Puerto Rican women of *West Side Story* (which opened in 1957 and ran concurrently with *Flower Drum Song* in 1960), a group of recent immigrants who sang a similar list of good American things in the song "America." The difference is the way Anita in *West Side Story* frames Puerto Rico as a place she never wants to return to. This never happens in *Flower Drum*

Song, where respect for the homeland is taken for granted and a multigenerational new-world community modeled on the homeland is in place. "Chop Suey," like the original *Flower Drum Song* as a whole, is about America now, a place where immigrants are fitting in, where their children are marrying for love, and where even the older generation can sing show tunes the larger white audience can enjoy.[13]

The 2002 revisal retained the 1960 setting of the original, and so *Flower Drum Song,* originally a contemporary story, became a period piece. Hwang's version cuts the entire citizenship scene, along with the original's evocation of a solid middle-class Chinese American world with stable ties to the homeland. Instead, Hwang denies his characters any anchor in the new world. "Chop Suey" becomes the act two opener at the "Club Chop Suey." All Hammerstein's references to 1950s America were removed and the number redesigned along the lines of "Wilkommen," the decadent opening of *Cabaret* (1966). Uncle Sammy—an elder Chinese transformed from traditional opera singer to nightclub emcee—brings on the boy waiters and girl dancers, the latter dressed as dancing "to go" containers and introduced with the cry "And don't forget MSG for More Stunning Girls." All the sensitivity of the original is lost in this generic Broadway spectacle, where funny costumes stand in for Hammerstein's lyrics (which were perhaps too specific in their references to strike a chord with twenty-first-century audiences).

While domestic spaces dominate in the original, Hwang turned *Flower Drum Song* into a backstage musical where cultural tensions between Chinese and American values were dramatized as a contrast between traditional Chinese opera and the brash sounds of a Chinese-themed nightclub in 1950s San Francisco Chinatown.[14] While this conceit may work on a dramatic level, musically it proves problematic. Hwang had no access to music of a remotely authentic Chinese kind: he was limited to Rodgers's score. Rodgers's tunes for *Flower Drum*

Song are largely unmarked by exotic "Oriental" tropes: only Mei Li's songs contain such touches. *Flower Drum Song* sounds, especially in its melodies, for the most part like a typical Rodgers and Hammerstein score. Preserving the potential for most of the songs to be sung out of context, Hammerstein seldom referred to the Chinese identity of the characters in his lyrics. The discrete addition of "Oriental" colors by orchestrator Robert Russell Bennett renders the score just slightly foreign. For the revisal, orchestrator Don Sebesky imported a small battery of instruments, mostly percussion, from the Peking opera tradition into the pit orchestra. These striking timbres are carefully introduced at the start of the revisal, giving the opening moments an exciting otherness (⬤ Example 1.6). Still, these often delicate sounds do little to alter the forceful showbiz quality of the whole. When traditional Chinese opera is demonstrated with the tune "You Are Beautiful," Chinese flute and gongs are given prominence, but the tune is firmly in the Broadway tradition and the vocal style of the performers draws on the emotive power ballads of Broadway megamusicals and animated Disney films (⬤ Example 1.7). Under these terms, the music cannot contribute to the storytelling or delineation of character. This didn't matter much in Hammerstein's version, which presents a world where assimilation is the goal and continuity with Broadway tradition is emphasized. But in the revisal, where stylistic contrast between traditional Chinese and American show biz is key, there simply isn't enough musical difference available in the Broadway idiom to make the point.[15]

ADDING THE BLACK GOSPEL VOICE IN 1990S REVISALS

Asians and Latinos have been less important in the history of the musical primarily because their occasional inclusion has not had a lasting impact on the music or dance content of the genre. In sharp contrast, identifiably African American musical styles have had, and continue to have, a formative impact on the sound of the musical. This is apparent in a minor trend of 1990s and 2000s revivals: the introduction of featured black characters into shows that were originally all white. In the film version of *Chicago* (2002), for example, rapper turned mainstream star Queen Latifah transformed warden Mama Morton into a blues queen. This felicitous casting decision allowed the 1920s figure of the blues queen—such as Bessie Smith—to find a place in a book musical. A white actress could not have used the song "When You're Good to Mama" to invoke the classic blues the way Latifah does. She draws effectively on both the cultural memory of the blues queens and her own past as a truth-telling female rapper. The highly theatrical nature of *Chicago*'s narrative and the anti-realistic nature of the musical as a genre permit Latifah to use her bona fide star power to play an authority figure with little period dissonance—although, clearly, a black woman working in a Chicago prison in the 1920s would not have been the warden. (The long-running 1996 Broadway revival of *Chicago* has featured several black women in the role of Mama Morton. Indeed, every major role has been taken by a performer of color at some point in the twenty-year span of the production, even though the original cast, with the exception of one supporting member, was entirely white.)

Latifah's performance doesn't substantially alter the musical style of *Chicago*, which sounds like any number of Broadway scores evoking the 1920s. In a more transformative strategy, Broadway revisals of *Grease* (1994) and *How to Succeed in Business Without Really Trying* (1995) introduced black performers and gospel vocal style into shows that originally lacked both. In "Beauty School Dropout" from *Grease*, the falsetto stylings of the original Teen Angel were transformed into a ten-minute production number led by Billy Porter, who would go on to record the role of the soul-singing James Thunder Early in a live concert version of *Dreamgirls*. The original "Beauty School Dropout" was a Ziegfeldian costume parade, with girls parading around to the accompaniment of a singer channeling white 1950s teen idols such as Paul Anka. Casting a black gospel voice as the Teen Angel for the revival, "Beauty School Dropout" was turned into an ecstatic black revival production number fully twice the length of the original. (Porter's replacements in the long-running production were all black performers: men and women; several of whom, such as Chubby Checker and Darlene Love, brought pop music fame as an extratextual dimension to their featured appearance in one scene.) In the revival of *How to Succeed in Business Without Really Trying*, African American actress Lillias White played the role of executive secretary Miss Jones. In the original, Miss Jones was a prim older white woman who let loose her operatic top notes while dancing on the boardroom table in the eleven o'clock number "Brotherhood of Man"—the joke of Miss Jones's presence as the only woman in the number turned on the sudden evaporation of her staid, self-possessed character (◑ Example 1.8). In the revisal, White as a black Miss Jones quickly takes control of the number by musical means. As the only black person in the room—by Broadway logic, she's the only one who's "got rhythm"—White alters the meaning of "brotherhood" and recasts the scene as a gospel number. She teaches the rhythmically challenged white executives how to clap off the beat and leads them in some cries of "sistah" in addition to all the "brothers" being passed around. The musical highlight—of the scene and arguably the show—comes when White takes the lead vocal, riffing on the song in a Broadway-gospel idiom (◑ Example 1.9) introduced most successfully in the black-cast musical *Dreamgirls* (1981). Broadway audiences for the *How to Succeed* revival would have known White's past roles—she played Effie in the 1987 revival of *Dreamgirls*—and they certainly would have anticipated her singing in her characteristic "black" style: why else would White be cast at all? Having to wait until almost the end of the show, and then hearing White let loose in only one number, proves to be the price exacted by a stage musical tradition that has so thoroughly and for so long invested in maintaining the color line.

NOTES

1. "Rodgers, Hammerstein Reply to Lee Newton on 'Show Boat'" (*Daily Worker* [October 25, 1948]: 13).
2. See chapter 2 in Andrea Most, *Making Americans: Jews and the Broadway Musical* (Cambridge, MA: Harvard University Press, 2004).
3. See chapter 5 of Sophie Tucker, *Some of These Days: The Autobiography of Sophie Tucker* (Garden City, NY: Doubleday, Doran and Company, 1945).
4. Part two of Raymond Knapp, *The American Musical and the Formation of National Identity* (Princeton, NJ: Princeton University Press, 2005) considers the nation-making functions of the genre in detail.
5. See also Warren Hoffman, *The Great White Way: Race and the Broadway Musical* (New Brunswick, NJ: Rutgers University Press, 2014).
6. Jules Bledsoe, another black singer on the New York scene, introduced Joe and "Ol' Man River" in the original production of *Show Boat*. For more on the song and its use by Robeson and others, see Todd Decker, *Who Should Sing 'Ol' Man River': The Lives of an American Song* (New York: Oxford University Press, 2015).
7. For a comprehensive consideration of the original production, stage revivals, and film versions of *Show Boat*, see Todd Decker, *Show Boat: Performing Race in an American Musical* (New York: Oxford University Press, 2013). For *Show Boat*'s important and changing place in the historiography of the Broadway musical, see Todd Decker, "'Do You Want to Hear a Mammy Song?': A Historiography of *Show Boat*" (*Contemporary Theatre Review* 19.1 [2009]: 8–21).

8. The 1973 Broadway musical *Raisin* offers a rare example of a musical play examining African American contemporary life in a serious yet commercially viable manner.

9. Lisa Shaw, *Carmen Miranda* (London: BFI, 2013) considers the resonance of Miranda's use of Portuguese as, in part, an appeal to her Brazilian fans, who had a complicated relationship to her Hollywood fame and persona.

10. Horne appeared in two films prior to her MGM contract: *The Duke is Tops* (1938, made by Million Dollar Productions, a small white-owned independent studio producing films for black audiences) and the musical short *Boogie-Woogie Dream* (1941; released 1944).

11. For a detailed analysis of Horne's film career, especially her many MGM solos, see Richard Dyer, *In the Space of a Song: The Uses of Song in Film* (New York: Routledge, 2012), chapter 6.

12. The megamusical hit *Miss Saigon* was imported from London.

13. This is not to imply that Asian Americans have not had a conflicted relationship with *Flower Drum Song*'s representation of Chinese characters and culture. As the only prominent stage or film musical about the Asian American experience, the show has been widely discussed and often excoriated.

14. These two entertainment traditions were indeed opposing each other in Chinatown at the time.

15. For an opinionated history of both versions, see David H. Lewis, *Flower Drum Songs: The Story of Two Musicals* (Jefferson, NC: McFarland, 2006).

2

Gender and Sexuality

STACY WOLF

■ □ ■

THE REPRESENTATION AND PERFORMANCE OF gender and sexuality[1] in musicals function as building blocks as basic to the form as song, dance, script, or design. Whether or not a musical seems to be "about" gender or "about" sexuality, these axes of identity invariably organize a musical's message, its ideological work, and its emotional effects, since all of the characters in a musical can be identified and analyzed in terms of their gender and sexuality.[2] We can ask, What do the characters, as male and female, do in the story? What do they sing? How do they move? How do they relate to one another as men and as women? How are characters' sexualities embodied and envoiced in a musical? What is the effect of characters' sexualities on the musical? Like any identity written on the body, gender and sexuality operate semiotically; actors and audiences rely on culturally and historically specific images of gender and sexuality to interpret characters, their actions, behaviors, and desires. Moreover, a character, as written on a page in words and musical notes and as inhabited by a performer who sings, dances, and acts, comprises innumerable additional identity categories, such as race, ethnicity, age, and even the body's shape and size. What emerges in the musical as a character's "personality" is insepa-rable from these identity categories.

This chapter offers several frameworks for analyzing gender and sexuality in musicals. With expanding spheres of focus, I first consider characters in themselves, or character types. I then look at characters in relation to one another, both within and across genders, and especially, the heterosexual couple, the figure that fundamentally organizes most musicals. I then move from text to performance, to examine the contradictions that bubble up when a role is embodied; the varying interpretations that actors bring to a given role; and the different readings that materialize at specific historical moments. At the end of the chapter, I briefly connect gender and sexuality to the musical as a genre.[3]

CHARACTERS AND CHARACTER TYPES

Characters in musicals are drawn in broad strokes. As Lehman Engel puts it, "Characters are always (to the au-dience) precisely who and what they seem to be."[4] Thus, characters as gendered fall into types, and often according to vocal range. For women, these include the ingénue, typ-ically a soprano, such as Christine in *The Phantom of the Opera* or Marian in *The Music Man*; the comic sidekick, or bitch, or witch, typically a mezzo, such as Aldonza in *Man of La Mancha* or Sally in *Urinetown*. Altos are some-times middle-aged principals, such as Rose in *Gypsy* or Mrs. Lovett in *Sweeney Todd*, or older character roles, such as Mme. Armfeldt in *A Little Night Music*.[5] Although many male romantic leads are tenors, such as Tony in *West Side Story* and the title character in *Pippin*, male roles are less typecast by vocal range than women's.

While every character is gendered, some musicals actually present the process of becoming gendered as the central narrative. *Gypsy*, for example, follows Louise from a disregarded tomboy who plays the back end of a cow to a rich and successful stripper. The story of the character's development—how she comes of age and finds her identity—is her gendering, or the process by which she becomes a woman. In addition, many mid- and late-twentieth-century musicals elide the process of becoming gendered with that of becoming heterosexual. Both *Funny Girl* and *The Sound of Music*, for example, feature central female characters, Fanny Brice and Maria, who begin as independent and somewhat childlike, and move toward romance and heterosexual coupling over the course of the musical.

The Sound of Music's story is Maria's Bildungsroman. As she comes to understand her life's true calling, she moves from one idealized image of "Woman" to another, occupying over the course of the musical the two stereotypical edges of the good feminine: nun/virgin and wife/mother. The musical wants the audience to see this process as Maria's natural, inevitable maturation from tomboy to woman. She was never meant to be a nun anyway, the musical argues, and her protestations to falling in love, which she enacts by leaving the von Trapp household and returning to the abbey at the end of act 1, emphasize both her guilelessness and the naturalness of her attraction to Captain von Trapp. The musical equates Maria's being a nun with entrapment (even though the nuns are portrayed as warm, good-humored, and intelligent) and being a mother and wife (especially of children who are nearly grown, and of a very wealthy man) with freedom and worldliness, albeit an unpretentious and tempered sociability compared to that of the Baroness.

From a feminist perspective, Maria's trajectory is ultimately narrowing and conservative; she sacrifices her independence to be a mother. On the other hand, a feminist reading also observes that Maria makes her own choices and transforms the entire von Trapp household: she redirects the children's bad behavior by channeling their energy into play and music and reopens Georg to music and feeling. Maria, the star, dominates the family and the musical alike.[6] In contrast to Fanny Brice, whose marriage fails because she insists on staying in show business even when Nick is arrested (implying that Fanny wasn't an appropriately dutiful wife in the first place since she failed to protect her man), Maria's marriage succeeds because she gladly becomes a (step)mother and leads her family to freedom. The tone of each musical's ending, one tragic and one triumphant, corresponds to Fanny or Maria's matrimonial, or heterosexual, success. Like *Sweet Charity* and *Cabaret* on the tragic side, and *Guys and Dolls* and *The Music Man* on the triumphant side, *Funny Girl* and *The Sound of Music* naturalize the affiliation between maturity and heterosexual romance.[7]

Similarly, men in some musicals embark on a performative journey that intertwines gender and sexuality and moves from homosocial to heterosexual, from their buddies to a wife. Examples include Tony in *West Side Story*, Marius in *Les Misérables*, and Sky and Nathan in *Guys and Dolls*. Through the force of the narrative, told insistently in song and dance and script, many musicals convey the ideological message that proper maturity is becoming feminized/masculinized. Moreover, proper feminization/masculinization is inseparable from heterosexual awakening. In this way, musicals tie together psychological development, gender, and (hetero)sexuality.

Still, characters in many musicals are coded as gay, such as Moonface Martin in *Anything Goes*, Randy Curtis (first played by Danny Kaye) in *Lady in the Dark*, Henry Higgins and Pickering in *My Fair Lady*, the tomboy Anybodys in *West Side Story*, and to some commentators, Robert in *Company*.[8] Gay-signifying men in musical films include, for example, Adam (played by Oscar Levant) in *An American in Paris*, Cosmo

Brown (played by Donald O'Connor) in *Singing in the Rain*, and Max (played by Richard Haydn) in *The Sound of Music*. Explicitly gay characters appear in the films *Cabaret, The Rocky Horror Picture Show*, and *Victor/Victoria*, and on stage in Jerry Herman and Harvey Fierstein's *La Cage Aux Folles* and William Finn's *Falsettos*, to name a few. A bevy of short-lived adult musicals sprang up in the 1970s, such as *Let My People Come*, which included gay characters for social activist as much as art-making purposes.[9] More typically, though, until the mid-1990s, when an explicitly gay character appeared in a musical, he (and it was almost always a man) had to bear the burden of representation, signifying more than simply an individual character, standing in for the very idea or whole category of gay people.

A *Chorus Line*, for example, introduced several characters (all men) who admitted they were gay, but only one whose story was told in detail. Paul's confessional monologue forms the emotional climax of *A Chorus Line*. What does Paul's gay identity mean in the musical? In an extended spoken "scene" near the end of the musical, Paul tells the heartbreaking story of his parents' discovery that he was performing in a drag show. He explains that, during the final show before the company went on tour, his parents came to the theater to say good-bye. They arrived too early and recognized him dressed as a woman. As Paul relates the story, "So I took a deep breath and started down the stairs and just as I passed my mother I heard her say: 'Oh my god.'" Stunned and horrified, his parents still stand by him, as Paul tells it, and his father commands the producer, "Take care of my son"; it's the first time he has referred to Paul as his son. By the end of the monologue, Zach, the director of the unnamed musical for which the characters in *A Chorus Line* are auditioning, and the lone witness to the story, comes onto the stage for the first time since the opening scene and puts his arm around

Paul. This kind and sympathetic gesture is Zach's only one in the show, and compared to his shrugging cruelty toward Cassie, his ex-lover, it at once suggests his humanity as well as his homosocial (if not homosexual) affiliation. For the theater audience, Zach's attention and onstage appearance underline the importance of this moment and invite sympathy toward a gay character, too. During the next section of the audition, however, Paul's knee gives out, eliminating him from contention. The musical at once values, rouses sympathy for, and punishes the gay character.

Paul's ethnic identity as Puerto Rican is equally significant and inseparable from his homosexuality in *A Chorus Line*.[10] He is stunned that his traditional parents embrace him, and their steadfastness makes his story even more potent, since it suggests that he is such a sweet and loving son that his parents can't desert him in spite of his being gay. All of the characters in *A Chorus Line* identify themselves by their hometown per Zach's opening gambit, often referring to race and ethnicity. The significance of race and ethnicity in this 1975 musical reflects the era of its birth, when the push for racial and ethnic equality was very much a part of U.S. culture. Diana's charming and devastating solo, "Nothing," recounts her failure to do "improvisation" in an acting class, which she blames as much on her being Puerto Rican ("they don't have bobsleds in San Juan!") as on her skepticism of the whole enterprise. When Richie announces, "I'm black," it plays as a joke in the musical because he is visibly African American.

Although *A Chorus Line* writes characters' races and ethnicities into their lines and songs, every character in every musical is racialized, whether or not race is marked, and a character's race/ethnicity inflects what gender and sexuality mean at every turn. In some musicals, racial or ethnic identity is part of the very fabric of the story. For example, in *West Side Story*, Anita seems sexually available to the white boys in Doc's drugstore because they see her as a "spicy Latina"; in *The King and I*, Anna can challenge the King of Siam because she is an educated white woman and he is a "primitive" Asian man; in *Fiddler on the Roof*, Tevye is confronted with diminishing patriarchal power as a Jewish man; in *The Color Purple*, Celie's financial and emotional independence are extraordinary because she is an African American woman; in *In the Heights*, Nina struggles to adjust to Stanford because she is Latina. Moreover, in each example, the significance of a character's race/ethnicity is historically specific, both in relation to the musical's setting and to its time of production.

CHARACTERS IN RELATION: THE HETEROSEXUAL COUPLE AND HOMOSOCIAL COMMUNITIES

Heterosexual relationships, romance, and marriage provide the narrative spine of most musicals, typically the story of a couple's initial antipathy followed by a series of complications that eventually lead to their admission of love. Differences of origin, background, and temperament align with gender differences, and the musical's first duet, the subjunctive love song, foreshadows the couple's unification two or so hours later. In addition to presenting the meeting and mating of two characters of the opposite sex, the heterosexual imperative, or what Raymond Knapp calls the "marriage trope," performs Broadway musical theater's grander ideological project: to symbolically unite opposing forces in U.S. culture. When the couple admits their deep and abiding love for one another, their joining together represents a social, even political union. The ensemble's rousing finale in many musicals from *Oklahoma!* to *In the Heights* affirms how the couple is a synecdoche for the community.

Many musicals also introduce a secondary couple, sometimes comedic, forming a quartet of contrasting representations of masculinity and femininity. In *Guys and Dolls*, for example, the differences between men and women, signaled in the musical's title, is central to the plot. The musical concerns how "guys" and "dolls" occupy their own worlds and live by their own rules, but it also reveals how different guys and dolls can be from others of the same gender. Both leading men are inveterate gamblers, but that's all they have in common. The suave, elegant, but gentle Sky Masterson, introduced as the perpetual bachelor, sings two richly melodic duets with Sarah, the first the subjunctive love song, "I'll Know (When My Love Comes Along)" and later the openly romantic, "My Time of Day/I've Never Been in Love Before." Sky contrasts with the brash, bumbling, affectionate, and barely musical Nathan Detroit, Adelaide's longtime boyfriend, who sings only the opening of "The Oldest Established" and responds, half-speaking, to "Adelaide's Lament," "Sue me, Sue me, What can you do me? I love you." In a parallel construction, Sky unwittingly falls for and then seduces through a tricky bet and considerable alcohol the straitlaced, judgmental, sermonizing, Save-a-Soul mission doll Sergeant Sarah Brown, the musical's soprano ingénue. In contrast to Sarah, Nathan's match is the cold-afflicted, gum-cracking, husband-hungry, nightclub dancer and pseudo-diva, Adelaide. By the end of the musical, the women decide to accept the men's flaws, and the wayward men agree to marry, and with double weddings, the ensemble reprises the bouncy title song. The conventional architecture of two couples is also employed in, for example, *Oklahoma!*, *Wonderful Town*, *South Pacific*, *West Side Story*, *Bye Bye Birdie*, and *In the Heights*.

Another typical arrangement of story and romance occurs in triangulated relationships. Both Arthur and Lancelot compete for Guenevere's love in *Camelot*; both Curly and Jud Fry are in love with Laurey, and Ado Annie wants both Will and

Ali Hakim in *Oklahoma!* Other characterological triangles that also include queer affections include Henry Higgins, Pickering, and Eliza in *My Fair Lady*; Oliver, Bill Sykes, and Nancy in *Oliver!*; Cosette, Marius, and Eponine in *Les Misérables*; and Don Quixote, Sancho, and Aldonza in *Man of La Mancha*. While homosocial relationships abound, more explicit homoerotic (or actually gay) connections occur in contemporary musicals, such as *Rent*, in which both Mark and Joanne bemoan their mutual attraction to Maureen (and they sing "The Tango Maureen"); or *Wicked*, in which Glinda and Elphaba each have a crush on Fiyero (and by the end of *Wicked*, both Glinda and Fiyero are in love with Elphaba); or *Spring Awakening*, where Wendla and Moritz are both in love with Melchior. In every case, duets chart the weightiness of the relationships, and the musical's concluding tone conveys its ideological project.[11]

Homosocial groupings in duets, trios, and chorus numbers at once foreground differences within one gender and blur individual characters' differences under the rubric of the feminine or masculine. In "Matchmaker, Matchmaker" in *Fiddler on the Roof*, for example, Tzeitl, Hodel, and Chava sing a lilting waltz about their hopes for a husband whom the matchmaker will bring. In the song's half-spoken middle section, Tzeitl imitates Yente the Matchmaker and teases her sisters about the old and ugly men whom they'll be forced to marry. The song allows each girl to express her own unique fantasy and also underlines how they're all the same in their desire to marry. Just as the romance narrative of many musicals reinforces heterosexuality as the norm, single gender musical numbers reaffirm social norms, which for women in most musicals means desiring marriage. Still, in *Fiddler*, the 1964 musical that takes place in turn-of-the-twentieth-century Russia, Jewish young women choose mates that buck tradition. In *Sweet Charity*, which opened just two years after *Fiddler*, taxi dancers Helene, Nicky, and Charity sing and dance an exuberant, Latin-inflected number, "Something Better Than This," in which each outlines her escape from life as a sex worker, whether to marry rich or become a respectable secretary. Charity's friends ably articulate their dreams; Charity can't quite envision hers. Yet all three women sing the chorus and each takes up a verse to announce her fantasies, however formed or not. Bob Fosse's choreography is expansive, alternating airborne leaps and kicks with angry and determined cha-cha stomps. In *A Chorus Line*'s "At the Ballet," Sheila, Bebe, and Maggie, isolated from the others, each sing about how ballet became her refuge from a troubled childhood. The three women stand on a diagonal, their stillness contradicting the joyful motion about which they sing in soaring harmonies. In the background in shadows, the rest of the cast enacts their memories, practicing simple exercises and stretching at the barre. Like the trio in *Fiddler* and *Sweet Charity*, this number connects femininity with desire and longing, but here to escape to the world of ballet.[12] Other numbers that perform femininity include "America" in *West Side Story*, "Lovely Ladies" in *Les Misérables*, and "Junk" in *Spring Awakening*.

To date, no musical has simply replaced straight characters with gay or lesbian ones in a conventional structure. Stephen Schwartz and Winnie Holzman's *Wicked* comes closest, using the conventions established by Rodgers and Hammerstein and their contemporaries to create a feminist and queer musical. *Wicked* musically tracks Elphaba and Glinda's relationship from antipathy/attraction ("What Is This Feeling?") to common ground ("Popular") to relationship ("One Fine Day") to division ("Defying Gravity") to expression of devotion ("For Good"). While *Wicked* includes a heterosexual romance, a triangulated crush that both women have on Fiyero, and while Elphaba stages her own death and leaves Oz with him to pursue a heterosexual life, the end-run machinations of the plot hold less emotional sway than the sweetly wrenching final duet between the two women. In the final verse of "For Good," the women's voices wrap around each other, constantly switching voice parts and concluding the song in unison. The final dissonant chord of the musical, sung by the chorus, signals the community's dystopian state, since the proper romance has been denied. *Wicked* testifies to the flexibility of the formal conventions of the "Golden Age musical"—in other words, form doesn't determine content although it does determine narrative structure—and *Wicked*'s commercial success rejects the presumptive centrality of "boy meets girl."[13]

CONTEMPORARY MUSICALS AND GAY AND LESBIAN CHARACTERS

Rent creates new possibilities for characters' sexualities in musicals by representing multiple gay and lesbian characters with frank and casual openness. *Rent* is peopled with a gay male couple (Angel and Collins) and a lesbian couple (Maureen and Joanne) and it takes those sexualities for granted in the musical's world of NYC's East Village circa 1990. *Rent*'s structure—a single protagonist, Mark, surrounded by a close-knit community—borrows formal conventions of ensemble musicals of the late 1960s and 1970s, including *Hair, Company, Godspell*, and *A Chorus Line*. This structure enables the musical to nod to nonheterosexual identities and relationships, an ideological gesture that speaks to its (successful) intention to address musical theater's wide range of spectators and even make them feel politically progressive. This device of including a few gay characters in a community-based story is repeated with the gay male couples in *Avenue Q* and *Spring Awakening*, and perhaps foretells a musical theater future with a more consistent nod to gay people (or gay men, at least).[14]

Still, both *Rent* and *Spring Awakening* ultimately use gay characters to bolster heteronormativity. Angel serves as the emotional touchstone of *Rent*, endlessly generous and hopeful, caring and sensitive. All mourn his death, which compels the other characters to look at their lives and choices. That Angel's death enables the other characters to learn about themselves replicates a typical (tired) trope in which an Other (usually a person of color or a person with a disability) aids in the self-actualization of the principal character. Also, Collins and Angel have the most loving and healthy relationship, which the musical needs to eliminate so as not to valorize the gay male couple above all else. In addition, Joanne and Maureen sing a lively number, "Take Me or Leave Me," but the musical doesn't take their relationship seriously. Maureen is presented as a fickle, emotionally abusive, yet irresistible lover (Joanne and Mark's duet, "The Tango Maureen") and a less-than-accomplished artist (her "The Cow Jumped over the Moon" is a parody of performance art).[15] In contrast, Mimi and Roger's relationship lasts through the end of the musical, since Mimi comes back to life. This choice, one of the few that differs from Puccini's *La Bohème* (which provides the primary situational basis for *Rent*), shows how beholden twentieth-century musicals—even tragedies—are to the convention of a heterosexually happy ending.

Similarly, *Spring Awakening* offers a tacked-on celebrate-the-day ending that differs from its source material, even more jarring since it follows the suicide of one character and the death from a botched abortion of another. Like *Rent*, *Spring Awakening* affirms youth's hopefulness and the unstoppable passage of time, packaged with a seemingly progressive representation of homosexuality. Like *Rent* and *Hair*, *Spring Awakening* puts a male friendship in the center with a homosocial hue, heightened by Moritz's anxious and passionate admiration for and attachment to the confident, accomplished, renegade Melchior. The desire of the gay (male) characters, Hanschen and Ernst, is no more *verboten* than heterosexual attraction in the musical, as they repeat Melchior and Wendla's love duet, "Word of My Body." And yet, the gay scenes are played for laughs, with Hanschen a stereotype of a fey, arrogant cruiser. The presence of the gay couple effectively re-centers the straight couple as the norm.[16] A similar dynamic exists in *Avenue Q*, where the gay characters are sweet and silly but the center of the musical is Princeton and his love interest Kate. Even as these musicals show gay and lesbian characters, their ideological work is complicated and even contradictory.

In this way, these musicals' politics of sexuality echo earlier, pre-Stonewall musicals in which the gay-seeming characters, always part of the theatrical world, force sympathy and iden-tification onto the heterosexual couple.[17] Typically, these queer characters sing little or not at all. In *The Sound of Music*, for example, Max is a gay stereotype (and perhaps Jewish, even though he is for a time accommodating to the Nazis), singularly obsessed with the niceties of life and a successful public image and not the least bit romantically interested in women. He is the friend/sidekick who is never a threat to the leading man. Nor is he a match for Elsa, the Baroness, who calls up her own vampirish lesbian stereotype. The queer presence of Max and Elsa sharpen the inevitability of Maria and Georg's union.[18] For a given musical, then, it's not enough to merely identify gay or gay-seeming characters; one should also consider what those characters do and how their existence and their actions con-tribute to the overall meaning and effect of a musical.

EMBODIED CONTRADICTIONS

While considerable information about gender in a musical can be gleaned from a script and a score, for audiences, musicals consist of embodied performances in real time. Performance analysis acknowledges this reality by examining what the men and women actors actually do over the course of the show. How often is the performer on stage? How many songs does she sing or dance and what kinds of songs and with whom? How, when, and with whom does he occupy space on the stage in song, dance, or spoken scene? While the script specifies such details, only in performance can an audience feel the dynamic effects of space, kinesthetics, and time, as well as the actor's performance choices and presence.

Dance's aestheticized, formalized movement, typically more symbolic than mimetic, defines gender as well. Diegetic waltzes in *Cinderella, The Sound of Music,* and *My Fair Lady,* mambo, jitterbug, and cha-cha in *West Side Story* ("The Dance at the Gym"), and athletic modern dance in *Wicked* ("Dancing through Life") also provide scenes of many bodies moving, enabling the couple to form through choreography. Other dances within single gender groups expand and define the meaning of masculinity or femininity, such as the Puerto Rican women in "America" as well as the male gangs, both the Jets and the Sharks in *West Side Story,* the nineteenth-century German schoolboys in "Bitch of Living" in *Spring Awakening,* or the jaded taxidancers in *Sweet Charity*'s "Hey, Big Spender," with each woman draped over a ballet bar in a unique pose of bored seduction, and then exploding in a rage-filled, gyrating frenzy of movement. Ensemble dance numbers such as "La Vie Boheme" in *Rent,* the extended "Hello, Twelve" sequence in *A Chorus Line,* or the opening number of *In the Heights* individualize the choreography for each dancer with movement vocabularies that express each character's identity.[19]

In some musicals, the onstage activities, or stage power, of the performer contradicts the written character's. The end of *Cabaret,* for example, finds Sally Bowles alone, having decided to abort her baby. Cliff leaves her to return to America, disgusted and fearful of the political situation and disappointed that she refuses to leave Berlin with him to marry him and raise a family. A "preferred" (that is, dominant or with-the-grain) reading of the musical sympathizes with Cliff, as the story is told from his perspective, framed (in the 1972 film version and the 1998 revival directed by Sam Mendes) by scenes of his arrival and departure from Berlin by train.[20] Over the course of the musical, Cliff grows from a naïve aspiring writer to a sharp observer of the Nazi's encroaching power. In the meantime, Sally's denial of the reality of the political scene is conflated with her refusal to marry Cliff: the musical frames both choices as her avoidance of reality, her immature, unreasonable resistance to conventional options. *Cabaret* presents Sally's insistence on remaining single and a performer as childish, especially since she is not especially talented or successful. But the musical works against itself, because Sally sings numerous charming songs, dances in the Kit Kat Klub in alternating scenes, and is a vibrant, active character compared to Cliff's quieter, less musical presence. The audience, then, understands Cliff's choices but is more drawn to Sally. By the end, Sally's heartrending rendition of the musical's title song cements her stardom. Although *Cabaret* wants the audience to judge her, Sally's belting voice and charismatic presence demand that the audience adore her.[21] A similar dynamic occurs in *Sweet Charity* and in *Funny Girl*. These characterizations are not unrelated to the period when these musicals opened—the mid-1960s—and they exhibit extreme cultural anxiety about gender at the time, simultaneously demeaning and empowering their female principal characters. Significantly, although Fanny in *Funny Girl* does become a star, her Jewishness complicates her success; she is not "white" enough to be a real star.[22]

Like *Cabaret*'s treatment of the woman Sally Bowles, *A Chorus Line*'s treatment of the gay character Paul is contradictory. On the one hand, he is a main character and among the most memorable in the ensemble-based musical. When he admits his homosexuality, neither Paul's Puerto Rican father, nor Zach, the father figure, deserts him, which suggests his absolute goodness. Paul's beautifully wrought story takes up considerable stage time—a "number" made all the more effective for not being sung—and is central to the emotional movement of the musical. His subsequent injury is a key dramatic moment: it stops the action cold, compels Zach to ask the other dancers why they keep dancing, and leads into the penultimate number, "What I Did for Love." On the other hand, Paul is a victim in the diegesis, his emotion-laden story "kills" him and renders him unable to dance, to perform, to finish the audition. He cannot finish what he started. Moreover, Paul's account is the only one with heft in *A Chorus Line* that is spoken rather than sung or danced, in contrast to the powerful memories of the women in "At the Ballet," "Nothing," and Cassie's "Music and the Mirror," another emotional high point in the show. The musical implies that Paul's story is so raw and honest that it exceeds music and dance, but in the conventions of musical theater's languages, this choice of communicative mode shows how Paul can't fit in; he can't express himself in the languages that are valued here. That he is gay and Puerto Rican—two non-normative identities—the musical (perhaps unconsciously) suggests, excludes him from the white and heterosexual musical theater of *A Chorus Line*.

Rent also compromises its progressive intentions when the characters are actually inhabited by actors. Because Angel cross-dresses and the role tends to be cast with an actor who is slim and effeminate, he and Collins look remarkably like a heterosexual couple on stage. This performance choice normalizes homosexuality but denies its visibility.

The performative energy of musical numbers, especially duets or trios, creates intimacy between and among actors and deepens relationships from how they read on the page. *The Sound of Music*, for example, complicates its heterosexual romance story with the infusion of homosocial connections. The songs between Maria and the Mother Abbess, "My Favorite Things" (a duet in the stage version) and "Climb Ev'ry Mountain" (the latter's solo act 1 finale that includes Maria in its purposeful address), along with the thunderstorm bedroom scene between Maria and Liesl and their reprise of "Sixteen Going on Seventeen," all portray close connections between women.[23]

Contradictions that emerge in performance are also built into the conventional scaffold of musical theater's heterosexual romances. That is, a musical is indeed "about" heterosexual romance in terms of its meaning and ideological work, but that doesn't describe what is actually performed on stage. Because a musical represents the developing romance of its heterosexual couple through a series of obstacles and conflicts, it may, ironically, spend more stage time revealing how thoroughly incompatible the couple is. Heteronormativity and narrative conventions may naturalize the romance and its matrimonial conclusion, but often in contrast to what is represented on stage.

ACTORS AND GENDERED PERFORMANCES HISTORICIZED

Musical theater's history as a popular, commercial art form has meant that many characters were created for specific actors. Moreover, as Bruce Kirle has shown, exigencies of production, more than composers', lyricists', and librettists' idealized creative impulses, typically drive the creation of character and determine the details of a character's gender and sexuality.

An actor in a role simultaneously creates the character and re-creates her, giving the character body and voice, so that a character is ultimately inseparable from the actor who plays her. For example, Nellie in *South Pacific* and Maria in *The Sound of Music* were written for Mary Martin, accommodating her vocal range and offering particular musical flourishes to flatter her voice. Similarly, *Gypsy* composer Jule Styne wrote songs to play to Ethel Merman's strengths as a singer, so that later actors must re-perform songs composed for Merman.

When we talk about "Rose" in *Gypsy*, then, which Rose do we mean? Merman, who originated the "mastodon of all stage mothers," as the 1959 *New York Times* review described her, and whose voice is captured (albeit in a recording studio and not on stage) in an original cast album, and whose form is frozen in photographs (again, not from the performance itself but from a rehearsal specifically for photography)? Rosalind Russell, who made Rose permanent on film in 1962? Angela Lansbury, who performed the role in 1974 as librettist Arthur Laurents reimagined it (and directed it), bravely bowing beyond the audience's applause of the climactic "Rose's Turn" to reveal the character's slender tie to sanity? Tyne Daly, who revived the role to great acclaim in 1989 and gave Rose a new monstrous fierceness? Bette Midler, who brought a new Rose to audiences via film in 1993, ghosted by her campy star persona? Bernadette Peters, who, in 2003, found a vulnerable sexiness in the character that told audiences that Rose actually might have made a fantastic stripper herself? Patti LuPone, in a 2008 revival, again directed by Laurents himself, who, as *New York Times* critic Ben Brantley put it, is "a laser, she incinerates"?[24] Or Imelda Staunton, whose 2015 "tremendous performance" in London, which *Guardian* critic Michael Billington called "one of the greatest performances I've ever seen in musical theatre," "introduces infinite shades into the character"?[25] To parse out who "Rose" is, then, a scholar gathers information by listening to cast albums, seeing photographs, viewing tapes of performances, or experiencing productions live. These materials, whether heard or seen, or both, whether taped or live, compose the archive that laminates the performer onto the character. Gender and sexuality are envoiced and embodied in the person of the actor playing the character.[26]

Each actor remakes a character anew, and both actor and character are tied to historical contexts and the historically available performance of gender. For example, Nellie Forbush in *South Pacific*, as rendered on the page, in the score, and in Mary Martin's 1949 performance, seems more than a little tomboyish. Martin's angular, guileless affect, the lack of a duet between Nellie and Emile (due to Martin's refusal to pair her musical theater voice with the opera singer Ezio Pinza's), and the quiet concluding tableau of the new interracial nuclear family, subsumed the romance within the larger story of race relations. Nellie, then, could seem to be an innocent southern girl whose racism merely stemmed from her lack of experience in the world.[27] In the twenty-first century, though, even as audiences acknowledged the musical's World War II setting, when Nellie sings, "I'm only a cock-eyed optimist/ Immature and incurably green," she seemed dangerously like a scatterbrain unworthy of Emile's love. In the 2008 Lincoln Center revival, Kelli O'Hara's exuberant yet grounded portrayal of Nellie never compromised the character Rodgers and Hammerstein created, yet she emphasized Nellie's openness and her sincere curiosity, rather than stupidity. When O'Hara sang Hammerstein's lyrics, her Nellie was wisely self-reflexive. Without apology or embarrassment, she nonetheless conveyed the recognition that the character was aware that her sheltered life was a deficit that needed to be made up.

Other productions of *South Pacific* offer a range of historically based portrayals of the famous role, albeit on film and television. The 1958 film version, for example, features Mitzi

Gaynor as an excessively perky, not-very-bright Nellie, and the strangely hued scenes (director Josh Logan used tinted lenses to express the emotion of each scene) and awkward camera angles constantly remind spectators that the film is a relic, static and stagey.[28] Glenn Close played Nellie in a made-for-TV version in 2001. Not only is she older (a fact that rendered the character's naiveté unrealistic to some critics), but she is also serious and seriously convinced that each time she accepts or rejects Emile, it's for real. The different performances of femininity become especially clear in the famous "Gonna Wash That Man Right Outa My Hair" number. The Gaynor rendition, modeled on Martin's (both staged by Logan), consists of Nellie strutting around the stage, framed by the other women who mostly stand, sit, or kneel. Her minimal gestures include arm flapping and waving, and the song is capped off by the famous hair-washing scene, which Martin performed on stage eight times a week.[29]

Martin's performance, captured on tape for a 1954 television tribute to Rodgers and Hammerstein,[30] and Gaynor's both portray Nellie as trying to convince herself that Emile is wrong for her; both are light on their feet and tentative in their gestures. In contrast, with Glenn Close, as choreographed by Vincent Paterson, all of the women participate, sing, and dance. Using everyday props of buckets of water, hoses, and a clothesline, the women express group solidarity through joyful exuberance, singing defiantly that they will "wash that man right outa (their) hair." While the choreography still relies on mundane movements such as walking, strutting, and swaying, the women are physically grounded and interdependent, as sections of the song move across trios or quartets. In this version, Nellie is fully integrated into the community of women, who support her, sympathize with her position, and join her. The force of the ensemble, with Nellie in the center, renders the number a vibrant expression of female community, and Nellie's rejection of Emile, while temporary, seems committed and sincere. This Nellie is fully capable of taking care of herself and making decisions for herself. Without changing a word or a note or the era in which the musical is set, Close's version updated Nellie for 2001, just as O'Hara did in 2008.[31]

THE MUSICAL AS FEMININE AND GAY

While the musical continually presents performances of gender and sexuality as crucial aspects of character and so reinforces those social scripts, the form itself, as a genre, connotes femininity and gayness. Aside from the stereotypical and accurate observation that the musical is the cultural terrain of gay men, some of the most important, early analyses of the musical were written by gay men who argued that the very form of the musical is feminine and gay. D. A. Miller, in his evocative autobiographical tribute to the musical, *Place for Us*, writes that the dominance of women in the musical encourages a feminine, empowering identification for gay men. He describes the musical as "a form whose unpublicizable work is to indulge men in the thrills of a femininity *become their own.*"[32] In *Something for the Boys*, John Clum observes that many diva or strong female characters in musicals appeal to gay men, providing a feminine escape fantasy for those gay men who may not comfortably inhabit traditional masculinity. Clum finds musicals with explicitly gay characters ironically less compelling for gay men's identifications. Alexander Doty, whose *Making Things Perfectly Queer* takes on a number of cultural forms, of which the musical is one, writes that the exuberant performance style of the musical calls out to many gay men's sense of their own performances of gender. My study, *A Problem like Maria: Gender and Sexuality in the American Musical,* analyzes Mary Martin, Ethel Merman, Julie Andrews, and Barbra Streisand and the musicals in which they starred from a feminist and lesbian perspective. From a materialist and historical perspective David Savran links gender and sexuality to musicals' cultural stratification.[33]

Even as the terms, definitions, and performances of masculinity and femininity in culture shift and morph into bi, trans, queer, and so on, the musical remains reliant on bodies and voices, movements and sounds, characters, and performers alone and in relation. These categories of identity and presence will always constitute a rich and important area of analysis and interpretation for the musical.

NOTES

1. The keywords "gender and sexuality" might lead one, for example, to consider women and gay and lesbian artists of the musical. Other studies that take this approach include selected essays in *Passing Performances: Queer Readings of Leading Players in American Theater History*, ed. Kim Marra and Robert Schanke (Ann Arbor: University of Michigan Press, 1998), and *Women in the American Musical Theatre*, ed. Bud Coleman and Judith A. Sebesta (Jefferson, NC: MacFarland, 2008).

2. Although for the purposes of this essay, I understand gender and sexuality to be stable and recognizable characteristics, certain performance traditions play with such presumed legibility. Breeches roles, for example, cast women as men, and their appeal in part relied on male spectators' desire to see women's legs. Drag roles, such as the title role in *Hedwig and the Angry Inch*, stress the way that gender is performative and also critique gender's normalizing force. See, for example, Judith Butler, *Gender Trouble* (New York: Routledge, 1990). Though most musicals rely on the gendered binaries of masculinity and femininity, increased attention to trans identities will likely expand how gender and sexuality are represented and performed in musicals in the future.

3. The keywords "gender and sexuality" might lead one, for example, to consider women and gay and lesbian artists of the musical. Other studies that take this approach include selected essays in *Passing Performances: Queer Readings of Leading Players in American Theater History*, ed. Kim Marra and Robert Schanke (Ann Arbor: University of Michigan Press, 1998), and *Women in the American Musical Theatre*, ed. Bud Coleman and Judith A. Sebesta (Jefferson, NC: MacFarland, 2008).

4. Lehman Engel and Howard Kissel, *Words with Music: Creating the Broadway Musical Libretto* (New York: Applause, 2006), p. 229.

5. http://tvtropes.org/pmwiki/pmwiki.php/Main/VoiceTypes?from=Main.TenorBoy, accessed May 8, 2010.

6. For a longer discussion of *The Sound of Music*, especially in relation to Mary Martin, who originated the role of Maria on Broadway, and Julie Andrews, the film's Maria, see Stacy Wolf, *A Problem Like Maria: Gender and Sexuality in the American Musical* (Ann Arbor: University of Michigan Press, 2002).

7. *Gypsy* posits another, more ambivalent position. Louise grows up, but she is narcissistic, still trying to separate from her mother, and so not yet (properly) heterosexualized. In addition, Rose, the actual star of the musical, is singular and post-heterosexual. See Wolf, *A Problem Like Maria*.

8. For readings of these characters as gay-signifying, see Raymond Knapp, *The American Musical and the Formation of National Identity* (Princeton, NJ: Princeton University Press, 2005) and Knapp, *The American Musical and the Performance of Personal Identity* (Princeton, NJ: Princeton University Press, 2006).

9. See Elizabeth Wollman, *Hard Times: The Adult Musical in New York City* (New York: Oxford University Press, 2012).

10. Most of the commentary on Paul has focused on the conjunction of his being gay and Puerto Rican. See, for example, Alberto Sandoval-Sanchez, José, *Can You See? Latinos On and Off Broadway* (Madison: University of Wisconsin Press, 1999); Frances Negrón-Muntaner, "Feeling Pretty: *West Side Story* and Puerto Rican Identity Discourses" (*Social Text* 63 18.2 [2000]: 83–106).

11. One might parse out the specific dynamics of two different kinds of romantic triangles: one in which two characters of the same

sex vie for the love of a third person of the opposite sex, and one in which the pivotal character is currently homosocial but sees a heterosexual future.

12. Perhaps the feminine trio in musicals can be seen as a trope. As a trio, the women are less likely legible as "lesbian," and so are heteronormatively safer. These trios also depend on each individual's unique perspective, unlike the ensemble number that stresses community. Interestingly, many of these numbers express a desire to escape, while most ensemble numbers emphasize the characters' desire to belong.

13. For an extended version of this argument, see Stacy Wolf, *Changed for Good: A Feminist History of the Broadway Musical* (New York: Oxford University Press, 2011).

14. Gay-seeming characters also people the background of *Wonderful Town*.

15. The musical, perhaps unintentionally, expresses ambivalence about artists, since all of the art-making in the musical is bad, including Mark's film, Roger's song, and Maureen's performance art.

16. I saw the original Broadway cast with Jonathan Bradford Wright as Hanschen.

17. "Stonewall" refers to the Stonewall Inn, a gay bar in Greenwich Village and the location of the apocryphal birth of the gay rights movement. A riot ensued when police raided the bar and the gay and lesbian patrons fought back. On the history and significance of Stonewall, see, for example, Martin Duberman, *Stonewall* (New York: Penguin, 1993), and David Carter, *Stonewall: The Riots that Sparked the Gay Revolution* (New York: St. Martin's Press, 2004).

18. Knapp makes a similar argument in *The American Musical and the Formation of National Identity* (230–38). Also, the film centralizes the Maria/Georg romance event more by eliminating Elsa and Max's one song, "There's No Way to Stop It," a trio with Georg, from the Broadway version.

19. See Liza Gennaro, "Evolution of Dance," Chapter 4 in this book's companion volume *Histories*.

20. Among the numerous changes in the film version, Cliff is renamed Brian and becomes British and Sally (Liza Minnelli) is American.

21. For related discussions of *Cabaret*, see Knapp, *The American Musical and the Formation of National Identity*, and Mitchell Morris, "*Cabaret*, America's Weimar, and Mythologies of the Gay Subject" (*American Music* 22.1 [Spring, 2004]: 145–57).

22. For an extended discussion of single women in 1960s musicals, see Wolf, *Changed for Good*.

23. In the film version, the Mother Abbess delivers the news of Maria's new assignment without song, and Maria gains the solo, "I Have Confidence," which she sings during her journey. "My Favorite Things" is moved to the thunderstorm scene, and "The Lonely Goatherd" is added as a puppet show to emphasize how Maria fosters the children's playfulness and imaginations. See Wolf, *A Problem like Maria*.

24. Ben Brantley, "Curtain Up: It's Patti's Turn as Gypsy" (*New York Times* [March 28, 2008]), http://theater.nytimes.com/2008/03/28/theater/reviews/28gyps.html?8dpc, Accessed March 14, 2010.

25. Michael Billington, "*Gypsy* review," *The Guardian* (16 April 2015). https://www.theguardian.com/stage/2015/apr/16/gypsy-review-imelda-staunton-momma-rose-stephen-sondheim-jonathan-kent-peter-davison Accessed November 25, 2017.

26. Envoicing is, of course, a form of embodiment, and the body could be inferred from the disembodied voice. One might argue that Merman always and forever ghosts the role of Rose. On actors and ghosting, see Marvin Carlson, *The Haunted Stage: The Theater as Memory Machine* (Ann Arbor: University of Michigan Press, 2001).

27. This characterization would in no way excuse the character's racism, but it would place her attitude within a cultural and historical context.

28. See also Raymond Knapp and Mitchell Morris, "The Filmed Musical," Chapter 2 in this book's companion volume *Media and Performance*.

29. Martin became a representative for Breck shampoo, which suggests the visibility and importance of Broadway performers at the time.

30. The show was a "General Foods 25th Anniversary Show: A Salute to Rodgers and Hammerstein."

31. In addition, the earlier versions of the number, in which the women are weaker and less determined, read as more sexual and voyeuristic. In all versions of the song, the actor playing Nellie is subjected to the physical, real-life consequences of stripping, getting wet, and washing her hair in public eight times a week. While I put an optimistic, female-empowerment spin on the homosocial aspect of this number, such female bonding is also a well-worn trope of male heterosexual fantasy (cf. "June Bride" in *Seven Brides for Seven Brothers*), here underscored by Emile's catching enough of the final part of the number to parody it later.

32. D. A. Miller, *Place for Us* [*Essay on the Broadway Musical*] (Cambridge, MA: Harvard University Press, 1998), 90.

33. David Savran echoes many other scholars when he notes that "musical theatre. . . has in popular mythology been adjudged a sacred preserve of gay men" (59). See David Savran, *A Queer Sort of Materialism: Recontextualizing American Theatre* (Ann Arbor: University of Michigan Press, 2003). See also John Clum, *Something for the Boys: Musical Theater and Gay Culture* (New York: St. Martin's Press, 1999); Alexander Doty, *Making Things Perfectly Queer: Interpreting Mass Culture* (Minneapolis: University of Minnesota Press, 1993); Tim Miller, "Oklahomo! A Gay Performance Artist Vows that Musicals Shaped His Political Consciousness" (*American Theatre* 20.9 [2003]: 91–93); Wolf, *A Problem like Maria*. See also Matthew Bell's entry, "Musical Theater," in *Gay Histories and Cultures: An Encyclopedia*, ed. George E. Haggerty (New York: Garland, 2000), pp. 621–24, where he observes of the musical, "Perhaps no other modern art form succeeds so thoroughly in appealing, at the level of reception, to a gay (and implicitly male) 'sensibility,' and in refusing, at the level of denotation, gay content" (621).

3

The Politics of Region and Nation in American Musicals

CHASE A. BRINGARDNER

■ □ ■

ON FEBRUARY 28, 1999, AFTER eighty-five performances and thirty-six previews, *Parade* closed its run at Broadway's Vivian Beaumont Theatre. Retelling the story of wrongly accused Leo Frank, a southern Jew killed by vigilantes in 1915 in Marietta, Georgia, *Parade* struggled throughout its run to fill seats. Some reviews hinted at the difficulties audiences might have in embracing its dark material and dramatic innovations. Still, the short run was a shock, given that *Parade* was conceived and directed by Hal Prince, received generally positive reviews from critics, featured the work of Tony Award winning playwright Alfred Uhry (book) and promising newcomer Jason Robert Brown (music and lyrics), and went on to receive nine Tony nominations. But its failure on Broadway was overshadowed when *Parade* opened its national tour the following year at the Fox Theatre in Atlanta, Georgia, where it drew large audiences. Despite (or perhaps because of) its being based on a racially charged incident and its aftermath, recounting events that took place a mere twenty minutes from the theater itself, *Parade* exceeded expectations, becoming, according to local producer Christopher Manos, "a success in every way."[1] The positive reception of *Parade* in Atlanta not only gave the show newfound popularity but also drew wider attention to musical theater productions outside the traditional New York market, highlighting the urgency for scholars to think anew about how musical theater relates to ideas of nation and region, and the role of politics in reception.

NATION AND REGION IN RELATION TO POLITICS

The terms "nation," "politics," and "region" intertwine deeply. The very process of defining a nation or region is political by nature, since it entails drawing physical or figurative boundaries. For the United States, as historians Edward L. Ayers and Peter S. Onuf remind us, American geography "recapitulates American history," affecting and reflecting how individuals and groups have "thought themselves across space."[2] In defining a nation or region, one reorders and recontextualizes space, memory, and history through a recurring process of forgetting and discovery, resulting in a politically charged construct specific to one's contemporary historical moment.

Nation and region have often been used as contrasting terms. Nation, as defined by the *Oxford English Dictionary*, describes "a people or group of peoples; a political state," and comprises a "large aggregate of communities and individuals united by factors such as common descent, language, culture, history, or occupation of the same territory, so as to form a distinct people."[3] In the United States, ideas of nation developed during the time of the Revolutionary War and solidified during the writing of the Constitution. Good citizens of the nation, besides owing allegiance, believed in a shared national experience as documented in the Preamble to the Constitution, the basis for a communal understanding of "We the people." Yet political strife and unrest have continually challenged notions of a cohesive union. As a result, regionalism—that is, emotional or political affiliation based on smaller geographical areas—rose out of distrust or disbelief in the nation as a transcendent, unifying concept. Proponents of regionalism, then and later, located and defined identities within specific understandings of more local regions, in opposition to the national. Political conflicts such as the American Civil War resulted in part from these clashing projects of identity formation, with conflicts between nationalism and regionalism couched in terms of states' rights, sovereignty, and slavery. Such conflicts played out on both national and international stages and supported developing regional movements that continue to thrive.

Across the twentieth century, scholars increasingly used region as a historiographic vantage point, giving scholarly credence to political passions that had festered since the formation of the United States. Persuasive regional narratives established particular regions as distinctive and identifiable, beginning, as argued by regional historian Henry D. Shapiro, with Appalachia.[4] The "discovery" and popularization of Appalachia by scholars and the popular press at the turn of the twentieth century brought the region national and international attention. Appalachian studies identified specific traditions, practices, and rituals (moonshine production, musical heritage, etc.), celebrating the unique and untamed nature of the region in relation to the rest of the United States, while simultaneously grappling with the question of how Appalachian culture fits within American culture more generally. This successful model led scholars to develop studies of other regions, such as the South, New England, the Sunbelt, the Pacific Northwest, and the Midwest, which supplemented and sometimes contradicted national histories, presented alternative identity constructions to challenge traditional understandings of nation, and remapped discussions of space and place within an American context.

NATION AND REGION WITHIN MUSICAL THEATER SCHOLARSHIP

Within musical theater scholarship, few scholars have traversed the complex terrain where national and regional identities converge and diverge in the American musical. Many texts celebrate the musical as the first truly American form, citing its continued fascination with projecting, championing, and challenging the American Dream. Both John Bush Jones's *Our Musicals, Ourselves* (2003) and David Walsh and Len Platt's *Musical Theater and American Culture* (2003) position the musical as distinctly American and argue that it offers an appropriate lens through which to view American history. Both texts helpfully link the musical to America's own processes of self-identification and its struggles to understand its global position, establish itself as a land of opportunity, and sell itself as a paragon of modern culture.[5] Raymond Knapp's *The American Musical and the Formation of National Identity* (2005) argues that the musical has "helped us envision ourselves as a nation of disparate people, functioning within a world of even more extreme differences," and reminds us that while this project often appears to celebrate cohesion and sameness, musicals tend to construct and (most often) reconcile difference within an American "melting pot," as a hallmark of American identity. More broadly, Knapp argues that musicals "frame and embody larger political issues" and thus provide rich texts to be considered, dissected, and studied.[6]

Stacy Wolf's *A Problem Like Maria* (2002) and Andrea Most's *Making Americans* (2004) similarly see the musical as a key element of America's cultural history, but emphasize its pivotal role as mediator of American identity, cultural history, and politics. For Wolf, the musical is a place where alternative understandings of gender and sexual identity exist within and alongside more traditional understandings, whereas for Most, it has provided cultural space for Jewish artists to negotiate their roles and positions within American society and promote a more ideal America. For both, the musical creates, exhibits, and maintains alternative identities in the service of re-inscribing, refining, and restructuring American cultural identity.[7]

David Savran and Bruce Kirle further interrogate the American identity of musicals. In *A Queer Sort of Materialism* (2003), "Towards a Historiography of the Popular" (2004), and elsewhere, Savran argues for the importance of the musical as a site of cultural production, its position within cultural hierarchies and at the intersection of several disciplines, and—most germane here—its role in identity politics.[8] While arguing for a similar centrality of the American musical to national identity, Bruce Kirle's *Unfinished Show Business* (2005) envisions new historiographies of the musical that focus on regional identities in addition to national.[9]

As Kirle's work indicates, a focus on region provides an important counternarrative to the project of nation building and nationalism that frequently informs discussions of American identity. The openness of the text in musicals, coupled with their ability to offer multiple meanings at once, makes them useful sites for tracing conflicting cultural forces and for witnessing changing understandings of American ideas and ideologies. But while nation has received due attention in musical theater scholarship, region has not.

One exception to this neglect has been the frequent tendency to see New York City as the center of musical theater in the United States. Supporting this tendency is a narrative of exceptionalism that marks New York as particularly appropriate for the creation and development of musical theater, drawing energy from Manhattan's bustling streets, towering skyscrapers, bright lights, ethnic neighborhoods, cultural variety, and concentration of talent. John Kenrick's *Musical Theatre: A History* (2008), for example, cites New York's long history with theatrical production, its abundant spaces, its access to technological innovations, and its proximity to popular music centers such as Tin Pan Alley as some of the many reasons that New York proved ideally suited for musical theater.[10] Despite such attention to place and space, however, New York too often becomes a placeholder for the entire country, with its narrative of exceptionalism becoming one of substitution and even erasure: as New York City goes, so goes the country. Musical theater histories tend toward an unreflecting and often unconscious focus on Broadway, neglecting national tours and alternative centers of musical theater production.[11] Such histories, as well as those that ignore region altogether, underestimate the potential benefits of analyzing a musical and its production history from the perspective of region.

WHAT REGION OFFERS THE MUSICAL THEATER SCHOLAR

A regional approach to musical theater encourages readings that center on space and place and puts specific performances or musical texts in conversation with national and global productions. Regional issues are often present within the text or lyrics of a musical, as with *Lil' Abner, Blood Brothers*, or *Flower Drum Song*, in which case the narrative already identifies or implies a specific region for analysis, be it Appalachia, Liverpool, or San Francisco. Just as musicals provide audiences opportunities to reflect on debates over

American identity during various historical moments, they also offer them chances to reflect on regional concerns and identities as they relate to ideas of nation. From the Midwest identities in *Oklahoma!* and *The Music Man* to the various New York identities in *Guys and Dolls* or the immigrant communities in *West Side Story*, the American musical has frequently used regional or otherwise local identities to address larger political issues such as racism, exoticism, or tolerance. Examining the ways region functions within texts can lead to a more nuanced understanding of identity politics and relationships in musicals and thereby enhance interpretations and meanings for performers and audience alike.

A regional focus can also address the effects of space and place on a musical once it goes on tour or gets produced in local venues such as colleges, high schools, and community centers. After a Broadway musical departs New York City and begins an often multiyear journey across the country, the show's meanings may shift with each performance location. For example, the musical *Wicked* takes on a different meaning in Dallas in a venue located on the Texas State Fairgrounds from the one it has in a Phoenix theater in the middle of summer or in a Chicago theater in the winter mere minutes from the home where Frank Baum wrote *The Wizard of Oz*. Examining both national and regional reviews in addition to any available production notes, blogs, interviews, or other accounts can reveal the different ways a particular city responds to a touring show, which may allow us to see the show or the city itself in a new light. Regionalism provides a vocabulary and context for addressing the experiences of touring productions and for tracing how a show might continue to develop and shift in response to local circumstances. For example, references and intonations that resonate in one region may not translate effectively to another, as was the case with *Parade*.

Regionalism also provides additional rationale for the openness of musicals' texts. A musical does not merely replicate itself exactly from town to town but becomes like a living entity, adapting to the character and culture of the regions it tours. Considering the ramifications of, responses to, and rationales for a performance of *Oklahoma!* in Oklahoma City or of *The Music Man* in Iowa places each show in relation to other performances of the same musical in other cities. More important, such an approach finds as much value in interrogating regional productions as in studying Broadway premieres or revivals, in part because a regional focus disrupts the typically New York–centered biases of musical theater scholarship. Further, it offers a more nuanced context for examining the relationship between the text of a show and the particular audience in attendance, allowing for discussions of how meanings are formed and of how interpretations and understandings shift according to circumstance. How might a musical create meanings in a high school gymnasium in rural Kansas different from those of a production in the university theater in Lawrence or the large civic center in Topeka, and how do those meanings relate to the original Broadway production?

Furthermore, this approach will encourage us to consider the implications of shows created outside the Broadway system altogether, which work their way to New York City via out-of-town tryouts in distinctive other regions, such as the Pacific Northwest or the Deep South. We must think about how a musical originating in a repertory theater elsewhere in the United States—such as *The Color Purple* (Atlanta), *Shrek* (Seattle), *The Little Mermaid* (Denver), or *Passing Strange* (Berkeley)—might retain the flavor of that region. Through examining regional and national reviews, and production notes and narratives, among others sources, we can start to identify the traces of region that flavor Broadway productions.[12]

CASE STUDY: THE BEST LITTLE WHOREHOUSE IN TEXAS

To provide an example of what a regional approach might entail, I discuss *The Best Little Whorehouse in Texas* (1978) within a specific southern context. In approaching this musical from a regional perspective, I draw upon related work in American studies, cultural geography, and southern studies. Within American studies, for example, historian Pete Daniel (*Lost Revolutions*, 2000), reads the development of NASCAR and the Elvis craze, among other cultural events, as evidence of profound social, political, and economic changes in the South following World War II. Daniel explores NASCAR in the 1950s (including its moonshine-soaked roots), seeing it as a pastime that allowed traditional, God-fearing, lower-class Southerners to form communities of spectators that celebrated stock car racing in part as a refusal "to bow to the elite culture." Their support of the wild and often dangerous NASCAR, as opposed to the more refined racing traditions of Europe, indicated a "bending of culture to suit their purposes," thumbing their noses at larger national culture.[13] Thus, a specific regional cultural practice may be read as political resistance to the national. Likewise, southern scholars Gavin James Campbell (*Music and the Making of a New South*, 2004) and Tara McPherson (*Reconstructing Dixie*, 2003) emphasize performances in popular music, film, and television as sites where regional identities may be tested and contested. Campbell, for example, describes how productions by the New York Metropolitan Opera in Atlanta at the beginning of the 1900s "supplied a tune for a complex and sometimes macabre minuet between gender and race that only intensified after the Metropolitan Opera returned to New York."[14] Campbell emphasizes the way the Opera provided women and people of color a temporary opportunity to exceed their prescribed societal boundaries. McPherson argues that the television show *Designing Women*, while often perceived as progressive in its racial and gender politics, and while frequently addressing the "ways being Southern (of a place) intersects with being white, being a woman," remains trapped within a more problematic cultural hierarchy "where all the women are white, and all the blacks are men."[15] All of these examples provide models that easily translate to a musical theater context.

Traditional methods of musical theater analysis relegate *The Best Little Whorehouse in Texas* to a mere footnote in musical theater history, deeming it an unremarkable throwback to an older style of musical comedy. Conventional musical analysis would find that the show breaks little new ground aside from using a country-western sound, while a national analysis would erase the specificities of Texas and the South and let the whorehouse stand in for small-town America. Dance-based analysis, notwithstanding the lauded choreography by Tommy Tune, would tend to neglect the pointed political content of the book, whereas literary analysis might neglect to consider the preponderance of actual bodies on stage in a musical that revolves around the selling of bodily services. A regional analysis, on the other hand, addresses and incorporates many of these concerns while placing debates over regional identity at the center of discourse, thereby revealing the multiple layers of ideological construction within and around the show, and the multiple ways the show has conveyed meaning. Moreover, *Whorehouse* offers multiple layers for regional analysis: the text, the press surrounding the New York and several simultaneous touring productions, various audience responses to the touring show, and the subsequent Hollywood film.

Region dominates the musical's text (music and lyrics by Carol Hall, book by Larry L. King and Peter Masterson): "Texas has a whorehouse in it! Lord have mercy on our souls!"[16] In the small town of La Grange, Texas, "in the shadows of the state capitol," Miss Mona Stangley—madam extraordinaire—operates a whorehouse known as the Chicken Ranch, so named because during hard times desperate gentlemen lacking the standard three dollar fee could exchange a live chicken for the ladies' services (*Whorehouse*, 34). The local sheriff, Ed Earl Dodd, allows the whorehouse to operate both because of his love for Miss Mona and his perceived "small town" values of live-and-let-live. Melvin P. Thorpe, religious zealot and voice of the Watchdog radio program, however, makes it his personal mission to close the whorehouse and return morality to Texas. He enlists the help of the governor, a slick "sidestepping" politician more concerned with maintaining his power than serving his public (*Whorehouse*, 66). Meanwhile, the Aggies of Texas A&M have won a hard victory over the University of Texas and are treated—by a senator, no less—to an evening at the whorehouse as a reward for their efforts. The Aggies' visit marks the Chicken Ranch's last hurrah, as reporters and politicians then descend on it to close it down, forcing the women to leave, and Miss Mona to find a new home.

In telling the plight of Miss Mona, her employees, and her customers, *Whorehouse* places images of a southern traditional way of life against those of an encroaching modernity hell-bent on reform and change. These two opposing forces might be read as Old and New South or simply a simpler way of life in conflict with the speed and complexities of the contemporary. Historically, the concept of the Old South emerges in the mid-twentieth century in juxtaposition to the New South, an attempt to rebrand and reconfigure the region as a modern, civilized, and economically viable player in the national scene. The New South, according to historian Paul M. Gaston, relied on an image of the Old South as "poor, frustrated, and despised, because it had, by decree of history, become entangled in wrong policies."[17] To rescue the South from the depths of despair and ruin, New South proponents championed two main areas for reform: politics and religion. Yet in the musical, these two conflicting concepts of region take on different connotations. The Old South exists as the more desirable place, where people both mind their own business and maintain a sense of community through shared knowledge; thus, by tacit mutual agreement, the community remains silent about the whorehouse, allowing it to continue to operate despite the law. Conversely, the New South is configured as contemporary and over-mediated, reduced to two key terms or strategies: regulation and moralizing. These competing regional identities in the musical, reflecting actual political tensions, encourage audiences to reconsider traditional understandings of the conflict, so that *Whorehouse* can be read as a sharp, critical political commentary on southern regional history, with strong potential for progressive, transgressive performance.

Additionally complicating these contrasting regional identities is the setting of *Whorehouse* in Texas, which presents particular challenges to seeing the South as a coherent region. Some historians highlight "the ambivalence of Texans [to define] themselves as part of the South" and their preference instead to emphasize their independence; hence the nickname, the Lone Star State.[18] Yet others, such as Henry Grady, include Texas as a vibrant, prosperous part of the South in their work, praising the region for its contributions to a burgeoning southern economy through its profitable cotton and coal industries and linking its future to that of the entire southern region.[19] *Whorehouse* dramatizes this debate over Texas's inclusion in the South and links it directly to larger debates about the Old and New South.

These two ideas of the South are articulated early in the musical. When Miss Mona outlines the tenets of her business in her opening song, "A Lil' Ole Bitty Pissant Country Place," she details many rules and regulations for her girls, pointing to an idealized Old Southern regional identity in the construction of her ladies. Mona's rules on telephone usage, proper language, cleanliness, and general decorum assure a certain image for their customers, derived from a traditional antebellum picture of genteel, servile women, willing to please—the image of an alternative, reimagined older system. But Mona leaves space for maneuvering and some independence; in agreeing to "pay the food and the rent and the utilities" in exchange for their keeping "their mind on [their] work responsibilities," Mona allows the girls to maintain financial independence and a reprieve from the constraints of marriage and family (*Whorehouse*, 25). Through Miss Mona's business and its enactment of traditional southern ideals, these women embody the image of ideal southern womanhood while simultaneously defying social conventions and staking their own claims in a male-dominated society.

Positioned in direct opposition to Miss Mona and the ladies of the Chicken Ranch are Melvin P. Thorpe and the governor, the former a rabid religious reformer who wants to establish a new moral order at their expense, the latter a slick politician skilled in the rhetorical arts. *Whorehouse* uses Thorpe and the governor to emphasize the New South's desire to make the private public, as opposed to the Old South with its live-and-let-live attitude. Thorpe and the governor exist only within the public realm of the musical, always surrounded by large crowds of people, emblematic of their broad appeal and devoted followings. Their public personas highlight style over substance, typifying the overly mediated New South as presented in the show. These two public figures stand opposed to the private space and demeanor of Miss Mona's replication of the Old South.

Eventually, the New South regional identity represses and displaces the traditional Old South, as Thorpe's crusade compels the sheriff to close the whorehouse down. The New South imposes regulations and moral codes that replace the easygoing private roles suggested in Mona's house rules with a rigid hierarchical system with men on top, women beneath, and alternative identities eliminated altogether. With this bleak conclusion, the New South victory does not usher in a golden age; rather, its religious watchdog organization and corrupt political system simply destroys the Old South. True, men are re-inscribed as dominant, free to move about society; thus, the Texas A & M football team remain heroes despite their dalliances at the whorehouse. But the women must leave their home, abandoning their safe haven to face uncertain futures without the guidance of Miss Mona or Jewel, her assistant. In "Hard Candy Christmas," which they sing as they pack and prepare to leave, they do not sing about getting jobs or an education, but rather imagine, "Maybe I'll dye my hair," "Maybe I'll sleep real late," "Maybe I'll lose some weight," and "Maybe I'll just get drunk on apple wine" (*Whorehouse*, 81). They no longer have either the confidence expressed in earlier numbers or the independence to control their own futures.

For a musical that markets itself as a feel-good "musical comedy," *Whorehouse* leaves audiences with a rather forlorn vision: a nostalgic vestige of the Old South destroyed through corrupt political and religious figures embodying the influx of New Southern mentalities, who in effect "Northernize" the South through reform and governmental interference in a scenario redolent of post–Civil War "carpetbaggers." In the end, instead of simply celebrating a retrograde image of an antebellum South, *Whorehouse* offers a smart critique of the New South and its unquestioning enthusiasts.

WHOREHOUSE IN THE PRESS AND ON FILM

Newspapers and periodicals provide useful documentation of regional responses to particular musicals, offering box-office and production specifics as well as registering interactions with a given performance. For example, Clive Barnes of the *New York Post* recognizes the multiple forces at work within *Whorehouse*, calling it "a strange, old-fashioned, new-fashioned musical, full of simple sentiments, dirty words, political chicanery and social hypocrisy, decent jokes, indecent jokes, bubbling performances and music with a bustle."[20] Similarly, in the *Daily News*, Douglas Watt calls the musical "100% American," declaring it "both sunny enough and funny enough" to "change things with its cheerful disregard for reality" (Suskin, 93). Critics and audiences in New York responded to *Whorehouse* in a generally positive manner, refraining from painting Texas or the South as unsophisticated or banal. Reviews like these point to a feeling that the New York production presented a view of the region as down-home country. As Watt stated at the end of his review, "I'm only surprised they don't sell Girl Scout cookies in the lobby" (Suskin, 93).

Outside of New York City, reviews of the show begin to document the ways meaning shifted regionally. Ironically, one of the few negative reviews appeared in the June 1978 *Texas Monthly*, where W. L. Taitte criticizes the show for trying "to be too many things" and trying "to reach too many truths at once."[21] Taitte also reveals another level of regional critique, speculating, "When someone gets the gumption to mount a Texas production, I fear it is unlikely to be able to match the New York one, which is a model example of how to do a musical the right way." His frank assessment of the Texas theatrical community and its "more conservative institutional theaters" reminds readers that this musical, although created by Southerners, was workshopped and developed in New York, and thus has become a distinctly New York creation stripped of much of its potential to depict southern regional or Texan identities. In fact, he seems to argue that "real" facets of southern life, such as modesty and conservatism, will impede a straightforward presentation of the original material. Reviews such as Taitte's illustrate the possibilities of a regional analysis to deal with conflicting identificatory practices once musicals take to the road.

The press reaction to the Atlanta stop on the first *Whorehouse* national tour demonstrates how notices and reviews can help launch a regional analysis. Five days before its official opening, the *Atlanta Constitution* ran a series of articles about the production in the January 4, 1980, issue in an attempt to build audience investment in the production, thereby providing a performed interaction between the audience and the show even before it opened. One article, "Alexis Smith: Call Her Madam," profiles the actor portraying Miss Mona on the national tour and highlights her previous reputation as Broadway and Hollywood's "sophisticated lady"—almost as though juxtaposing this image to her role as Miss Mona will reassure readers that she is not actually a madam.[22] Smith is quoted as saying that the musical "has the greatest title in the world" (Litsch, 10-B). A companion article, "Atlanta Adds Spice to Salty Texas Comedy," profiles Amy Miller (portraying Ruby Rae) and Bob Moyer (newspaper man Edsel Mackey), emphasizing their ties to the city.

The final article of the series, "I Want Tickets to . . . Er . . . 'The . . . Ah . . . Best,'" recounts the hilarious experiences of the Fox Theatre box office in dealing with patrons embarrassed to say the title of the show out loud. Box-office manager David Stewart recalls people referring to the show only as "The Best," "that play," or "that show about Texas."[23] "I Want Tickets" also recounts the troubles the advertising campaign ran into during the show's New York run. Bus placards in New York had proclaimed "come on down to the whorehouse" but were removed by order of the City Council. Other venues required a new title altogether, "The Best Little Chicken Ranch in Texas." And public relations coordinator Warren Knowles is quoted as saying that "some radio and TV stations don't want the ads to run during prime time" (Litsch, "I Want Tickets," 1-B). But Atlanta had no such objections. Large print ads ran in the *Constitution* and television spots hailed its arrival. Atlanta's treatment of the show, especially its decision not to censor the marketing campaign, indicates a desire to be seen as more sophisticated than other cities on the tour, perhaps even than New York City itself. After providing a summary of the production history of the musical, the article concludes by heralding the ability of the show to "destroy the colorful language barrier," noting that "far into the hinterlands, well removed from the supposed evils of New York and Los Angeles, people are lining up to get into *The Best Little Whorehouse in Texas*" (Litsch, "I Want Tickets," 1-B). This final statement again makes a claim for Atlanta's sophistication and positions the citizens of Atlanta as active participants in projecting this image to the rest of the nation through their attendance at the show.

With the release of the feature film in 1982, only two years after the Atlanta premiere, *Whorehouse* entered a new phase in its representations of conflicting southern identities. Just as the Atlanta production had allowed the story of the whorehouse to reveal larger hopes and concerns for the city and region, the film broadens the story to encompass the entire South, primarily through casting. Rather than casting native Texans to play the roles, the film's producers decided upon Dolly Parton, a native of Tennessee, for the role of Miss Mona, and Burt Reynolds, a native Georgian, for the role of the sheriff (a part Larry L. King originally wanted Willie Nelson to play). Their participation in the film necessitated a wider understanding of southern identity since Parton and Reynolds were both already closely associated with southern identity, Parton through her music and Reynolds through his films, including *Cannonball Run* and *Deliverance*. Though the film was a box-office flop, its interpretation of the story, with additional songs by Parton (including

"I Will Always Love You"), contributed to its ability to be read as a commentary on the conflicting forces of an Old and New South. Parton's and Reynold's southern identities make the film a fascinating study in how an actor's identity interacts, in a complex negotiation, both with regional identities and issues of identity already present in a script or screenplay. For example, the interplay among Parton the serious movie actor, Parton the country music star, and Parton as Miss Mona illustrate the difficulties of reconciling an actor's regional identity with those of her character and of the musical itself.

While the theatrical production established more specific and nuanced embodiments of southern identity as it played before southern audiences on the stage, the film functioned differently in relation to region. The film, with its larger-than-life leads, saturated the southern identities in the piece and frequently treaded into an area of destructive caricature and exaggeration not present in the musical's original staging, while simultaneously sanitizing and cleaning up the material to suit a larger audience. Parton's larger-than-life personality coupled with Reynold's bad boy reputation exceeded the confines of their characters of Miss Mona and the sherriff, respectively, overshadowing any attempt at the subtlety and complexity of the stage musical. As Roger Ebert of the *Chicago Sun Times* observed, "The story has been cleaned up so carefully to showcase Parton and Reynolds that the scandal has been lost," replaced by "a hymn to romance"—a particular detriment to the film since critics almost universally cited the lack of chemistry between the leads as the film's chief failing.[24] For film audiences, the careful work of the musical to parse out a complicated ideological debate between Old and New South gave way to a star-studded, sterile romantic comedy between two extremely popular personalities—which is not to say that southern audiences may not have found pleasure or moments of identification in the film, simply that the level of discourse shifted. Moreover, the return to a more romanticized and caricatured version of the South only served to perpetuate negative stereotypes that the original musical had complicated and disrupted.

***

Seen through the lens of region, *The Best Little Whorehouse in Texas* becomes more than the sum of its bare mentions in musical theater history texts. *Whorehouse* stands at the crossroads of a debate between differing views of the South, grappling with the real political implications of national, regional, and state politics of the late 1970s. The Atlanta production of *Whorehouse* provides a particularly fascinating example of regional reception, reflecting residual tensions within that city concerning the New South project of reform and uplift. As the musical traveled state to state, region to region, from Broadway to Hollywood, it amassed an ever-growing collection of meanings that placed it at the center of a discussion about region and identity for those audiences in theaters across the country. In its travels from New York to Atlanta to Hollywood, in particular, *Whorehouse* gathered a variety of regional meanings and interpretations, beginning as an energetic, entertaining musical romp with southern flair, progressing to a lively debate between Old and New South mentalities, and coming to rest as a romantic star vehicle for two iconic southern personalities.

The wider implications of regional analysis for musical theater are rich and varied. Such an approach would unlock further avenues for the exploration of musical theater texts and of how they have different meanings for divergent audiences across states, regions, nations, and the globe. One might draw fascinating conclusions from comparing a production of *Oklahoma!* performed in Oklahoma City versus one in New York City, or a production of *Avenue Q* in New York City versus Las Vegas or Atlanta. A regional analysis of Baltimore productions of *Hairspray* might cast the piece in a different light and might reveal something about the city itself. A regional approach allows for an understanding of how a musical and its specific audience participate in the interpretive process for a show. By accounting for travel, venue, and identity (both regional and national), such an approach engages with the musical on an inherently political level as it positions the musical front and center in the processes of constructing, maintaining, and reconstituting cultural meaning.

NOTES

1. Dan Hulbert, "Theatrical Bright Side to Atlanta's Dark Story" (*Atlanta Journal-Constitution* [June 20, 2000]).
2. "Introduction," in Edward L. Ayers, Patricia Nelson Limerick, Stephen Nissenbaum, and Peter S. Onuf, *All Over the Map: Rethinking American Regions* (Baltimore: Johns Hopkins University Press, 1996), p. 1.
3. Oxford English Dictionary Online (http://www.oed.com/, accessed August 10, 2009.
4. Henry D. Shapiro, "How Region Changed Its Meaning and Appalachia Changed Its Standing in the Twentieth Century," in *Bridging Southern Cultures: An Interdisciplinary Approach*, ed. John Lowe (Baton Rouge: Louisiana State University Press, 2005).
5. John Bush Jones, *Our Musicals, Ourselves: A Social History of the American Musical Theatre* (Hanover, NH: Brandeis University Press, 2003), and David Walsh and Len Platt, *Musical Theater and American Culture* (Westport, CT: Greenwood, 2003).
6. Raymond Knapp, *The American Musical and the Formation of National Identity* (Princeton: Princeton University Press, 2005), pp. 7 and 283.
7. Stacy Wolf, *A Problem Like Maria: Gender and Sexuality in the American Musical* (Ann Arbor: University of Michigan Press, 2002), and Andrea Most, *Making Americans: Jews and the Broadway Musical* (Cambridge, MA: Harvard University Press, 2004).

8. David Savran, *A Queer Sort of Materialism: Recontextualizing American Theater* (Ann Arbor: University of Michigan Press, 2003), and "Towards a Historiography of the Popular" (*Theatre Survey* 45:2 [2004]: 211–17).

9. Bruce Kirle, *Unfinished Show Business: Broadway Musicals as Works-in-Process* (Carbondale: Southern Illinois University Press, 2005).

10. John Kenrick, *Musical Theatre: A History* (New York: Continuum, 2008).

11. Scott Miller's three "survey" books are an interesting partial exception, although his approach—offering focused discussions of shows that originated in New York, addressing themes and problems relevant to their being mounted elsewhere in repertory—rarely aligns with regional advocacy; see his *From Assassins to West Side Story: The Director's Guide to Musical Theatre* (Portsmouth, NH: Heinemann, 1996), *Deconstructing Harold Hill: An Insider's Guide to Musical Theatre* (Portsmouth, NH: Heinemann, 2000), and *Rebels with Applause: Broadway's Groundbreaking Musicals* (Portsmouth, NH: Heinemann, 2001).

12. A related issue concerns the "traces" that stem from authorship, which helps explain problems in reception, among represented constituents, of shows lacking such traces. Thus, we may note the troubled reception of *West Side Story* among Puerto Ricans, of *The King and I* in Thailand, or of *The Sound of Music* in Austria, which contrast sharply with how *The Music Man* plays in Iowa (book, lyrics, and music by Meredith Willson, a native of Mason City), *Oklahoma!* in *Oklahoma* (book derived, often verbatim, from *Green Grow the Lilacs*, by Lynn Riggs, a native of Claremore), or even *Guys and Dolls* to native New Yorkers (based on the work and language of Damon Runyan, Broadway's one-time authenticating voice).

13. Pete Daniel, *Lost Revolutions: The South in the 1950s* (Chapel Hill: University of North Carolina Press, 2000), p. 119.

14. Gavin James Campbell, *Music and the Making of a New South* (Chapel Hill: University of North Carolina Press, 2004), p. 65.

15. Tara McPherson, *Reconstructing Dixie: Race, Gender, and Nostalgia in the Imagined South* (Durham, NC: Duke University Press, 2003), pp. 35 and 187.

16. Carol Hall, Larry L. King, and Peter Masterson, *The Best Little Whorehouse in Texas* (New York: Samuel French, 1978), p. 34 (henceforward Whorehouse).
17. Dewey W. Grantham, *The South in Modern America: A Region at Odds* (New York: HarperCollins, 1994), p. 25.
18. Celeste Ray, "Introduction," *Southern Heritage on Display: Public Ritual and Ethnic Diversity within Southern Regionalism*, ed. Celeste Ray (Tuscaloosa: University of Alabama Press, 2002, pp. 1–37), p. 5.
19. Henry Woodfin Grady, *The New South, and Other Addresses, with Biography, Critical Opinions, and Explanatory Notes*, by Edna Henry Lee Turpin (New York: Maynard, Merrill, 1904).
20. Quoted in Steven Suskin, *More Opening Nights on Broadway: A Critical Quotebook of the Musical Theatre 1965 through 1981* (New York: Schirmer, 1997), p. 91.
21. W. L. Taitte, *"Tarts of Gold"* (*Texas Monthly* [June 1978]: 132).
22. Joseph Litsch, "Alexis Smith: Call Her Madam: Hollywood's Typecast 'Sophisticated Lady'" (*Atlanta Constitution* [January 4, 1980]: 1-B+.
23. Joseph Litsch, "I Want Tickets to... Er . . . 'The . . . Ah . . . Best'" (*Atlanta Constitution* [January 4, 1980], 1-B+).
24. Roger Ebert, "The Best Little Whorehouse in Texas" (review in *Chicago Sun Times* [January 1, 1982]).

4

Class and Culture

DAVID SAVRAN

■ □ ■

SINCE THE DECLINE OF VAUDEVILLE and minstrelsy in the 1920s, the Broadway musical has been the only form of American theater that could reliably be considered a part of popular culture. It is also the one form that has been exported all over the world and continues to be performed in Berlin, Buenos Aires, Seoul, and myriad other urban centers. It is the only form of theater to make a significant mark on mass culture in the United States and abroad and whose anthems, from "Ol' Man River" to "Aquarius," "Climb Ev'ry Mountain" to "Seasons of Love," are sung and listened to worldwide. In 1964, at the height of the rock–and-roll craze, Louis Armstrong's recording of "Hello, Dolly!" even managed to dislodge the Beatles from the number 1 spot on the pop chart. *The Phantom of the Opera*, meanwhile, with a worldwide gross of more than $3.3 billion, represents a landmark in popular culture.[1] And lest we forget, the dearly beloved Rodgers and Hammerstein musicals are performed countless times every day in countless languages all over the world. Yet to say that the musical is a popular genre engenders the question, "What *is* popular culture?" For the "popular" is always changing. As Bertolt Brecht remarked, "What was popular yesterday is not today, for the people today are not what they were yesterday."[2] And the notoriously slippery category "the people" can be, and has been, mobilized for myriad purposes. Usually when we invoke the people, we mean the middle and working classes, or at least certain fractions of these classes. But because the middle class that listens to Beyoncé is not the same middle class that attends the 2008 Lincoln Center revival of *South Pacific*, claims to the Broadway musical's status as part of popular culture have to be qualified, for both its production and consumption distinguish it sharply from cinema, television, and other kinds of what is usually called popular culture.

Surveys demonstrate that middle-class Broadway audiences have considerably more economic and educational capital than most Americans. During the 2007–08 season, the average annual income of Broadway musical theatergoers ($141,600) was roughly three times the national average. Spectators were, moreover, one and one-half times more likely to have completed college (26.3% versus 17.2%) and four times as likely to have had some postgraduate education (41.1% versus 10%).[3] But studies of audience demographics date back no earlier than 1981, leaving us only anecdotal information about the public that attended Broadway musicals for most of their history. This information, however, does correlate with recent statistics. We know that since the end of the nineteenth century—when musical comedy separated itself from burlesque, minstrelsy, and vaudeville, on the one hand, and the serious, legitimate stage, on the other—the producers and consumers of the Broadway musical have been mostly middle class. Although some of its makers, such as Irving Berlin and George Gershwin, grew up in working-class immigrant neighborhoods, the vast majority has come from middle-class families, and many, such as Richard Rodgers, Agnes de Mille, or Stephen Sondheim, from the upper reaches of that class. Audiences, too, must have had a good deal of disposable income, because in the early twentieth century, as now, the cost of admission to a Broadway musical was many times that of a movie ticket. In 1928, prices for musicals ranged from 50 cents to $6.60 and for nonmusical plays from 50 cents to $4.40.[4] (In contrast, 99% of the motion picture audience paid between 10 cents and 49 cents.)[5] Even today, a musical on average costs a theatergoer between five and ten times as much as a movie.

CULTURAL HIERARCHIES

To point out the Broadway musical's status as a middle-class phenomenon, however, only begins to analyze its relationship to popular culture. More important is to study how it has been positioned among forms of entertainment by its makers, audiences, and critics. Historians have pointed out that a clear-cut hierarchy of cultural forms did not become established in the United States until the end of the nineteenth century, just as musical comedy was developing its own distinctive character. It was during this period, Lawrence Levine reports, that the words "highbrow" and "lowbrow" were coined, the former "first used in the 1880s to describe intellectual or aesthetic superiority" and the latter, "first used shortly after 1900 to mean someone or something neither 'highly intellectual' nor 'aesthetically refined.'"[6] These terms, borrowed from a racially inflected phrenology, were used to accentuate the differences between a European-inspired, morally and spiritually uplifting art and an allegedly primitive, vulgar, commercialized art; the culture of the intellectual and economic elites (most of them of northern European descent) versus that of the working classes (many of them African Americans and recent immigrants from southern and eastern Europe). Opera houses, concert halls, theaters, and museums were constructed to look like classical temples to make certain kinds of art appear dignified—and completely dissociated from both the marketplace and the culture of the working classes. The older elite used the division between highbrow and lowbrow as a tool to organize and rationalize the social and economic realms and to buttress their own power. For in certain respects, the ability to fashion a hierarchy (cultural or otherwise) and police its boundaries is far more important than the specific content of categories like highbrow and lowbrow.

European concert music, opera, literary classics, and paintings by the old masters defined a highbrow culture at odds with an indigenous, turn-of-the-century popular culture. Then (as now) highbrow work tends to be wrapped in mystique, trading on its purported exclusivity, its authenticity, and its refusal to succumb to the commodity form. At the opposite end of the spectrum, captivating the largely foreign-born masses, were genres such as comic strips, jazz, nickelodeons, and, among theater forms, minstrel shows, burlesque, cheap vaudeville, and the like. Although these forms were not mass produced in the way that cinema was, they were usually deemed lowbrow insofar as they were imagined to be fit for consumption only en masse by the working classes. This period also saw the emergence of the so-called little theater movement in the United States, which tried to create a highbrow theater by producing the work of European playwrights such as Ibsen, Shaw, and Galsworthy. For the reformers of United States culture, this art theater was vitally important for elevating the taste of the theatergoing minority. Accordingly, it dedicated itself, as one critic then wrote, to "the encouragement and support of an American drama, the giving voice and tongue to a neighborhood, the production of the great masterpieces of the world, [and] the elevation of taste of the community."[7]

In 1909, the *New York Tribune* began to discriminate among theatrical offerings by ranking them in a clear-cut hierarchy, with "Comedy and Drama" at the top, followed by

"Musical Plays," "Variety Houses," and "Beach and Park." The most refined form, "Comedy and Drama," sold its orchestra seats mostly to "affluent audiences." The galleries, meanwhile, at least after 1910, were peopled by increasingly serious spectators, "earnest devotees of drama unable to afford orchestra seats," mostly "middle-class and mostly women."[8] Although no cheaper than "Comedy and Drama," "Musical Plays" thrived, attracting (then as now) larger and more diverse audiences. As developed by writers such as Irving Berlin, Will Marion Cook, and Jerome Kern, they adopted popular music styles—first ragtime, then jazz—and elaborated their own distinctive brand of romantic comedy punctuated by song, dance, and shtick. Yet musical comedy and musical revue—part play, part variety; part narrative, part spectacle; part drama, part song and dance; part opera, part "leg" show; part art, part glamour—have always been hybrid genres that resist easy categorization. The *Tribune*, for example, classified a high-toned revue like the Ziegfeld Follies not as variety but as a musical play.

The *New York Tribune*, however, was not alone in finding it difficult to categorize musical theater. Theater critics also were made uneasy by the lack of a clear boundary between variety entertainments and the legitimate stage, between "whipped cream" and the "roast."[9] Burns Mantle, the longtime editor of the Best Plays series, excluded musicals on principle from the "best plays" while another critic grouped musical comedy together with motion pictures and bedroom farces as genres that "dilut[e] the general average of intelligence and lower . . . the standard of demand" because they "are not yet really provocative enough . . . to tempt the taster farther into the theatre" (Sayler, 187 and 246). The dean of the critics, George Jean Nathan, was especially anxious that musical comedy know—and respect—its allotted position in the cultural hierarchy. An "outlet for our trivial moods," "the music show occupies to the theatre and drama the same relationship . . . that alcohol occupies to art: a convivial moment of forgetfulness." Problems arise when this amnesia-inducing tipple forgets its place and "takes itself with deadly seriousness."[10]

The musical theater—positioned between highbrow and lowbrow, between art theater and variety entertainments—has for almost a century epitomized the culture called middlebrow, an elastic category into which a great many artifacts can fall. The word was coined during the 1920s as a way of describing a rapidly growing species of art that emulated highbrow forms while attempting to make them more accessible. The middle-brow consumer was considered to be traditional at heart yet striving to be au courant, a middle-class man or woman with education and social aspirations who, Janice Radway notes, would "read the new book-review sections" in newspapers and subscribe to "innovative magazines like *Time* and the *New Yorker*."[11] Radway identifies the culture that attracted these people not as a "harbinger of new mass cultural forms" but as a distinctive by-product of American modernism, "a separate aesthetic and ideological production constructed by a particular fraction of the middle class offended equally by the 'crassness' of mass culture and by the literary avant-garde."[12] The middlebrow consumer was routinely described as—and condemned for—being a social-climbing parvenu trying to "pre-empt . . . the highbrow's function" and "blur the lines between the serious and the frivolous."[13]

The term "middlebrow" has generally been a mark of opprobrium, especially during the height of the Cold War (from the late 1940s through the 1960s) when the arbiters of taste were anxious about the position of United States culture vis à vis European highbrow art and eager that United States art should be as formidable as its military might. In April 1949, *Life* magazine published an article entitled "Highbrow, Low-brow, Middle-brow" that included a two-page chart that classified the public's taste in everything from clothes, drinks, and salads to entertainment, phonograph records, and reading. *Life's* article became so popular that pigeonholing one's brow level became "for many months" a "favorite parlor game."[14] This chart (which divides middlebrow into upper and lower) makes it clear that for postwar tastemakers, theater was *the* emblematic middlebrow art. *Life* puts it in the upper-middlebrow category (where it is designated by actors decked out in Shakespearean garb) along with *Harper's, Vogue,* and a dry martini. The pile of records in the upper-middlebrow's record collection includes Cole Porter's *Kiss Me, Kate* sandwiched between Chopin and Sibelius while the lower-middlebrow's includes Victor Herbert, Nelson Eddy, and Perry Como.[15]

The postwar critics were by no means the only ones to pigeonhole musical theater as a middlebrow form. Indeed, since the 1920s, musical theater has occupied what I would describe as an intermediate position in United States culture, recycling and recombining elements of, on the one hand, public amusements like jazz, vaudeville, and rock, and, on the other, more elite forms like opera and the serious play. Neither high nor low—or rather, *both high and low at the same time*— musical theater has consistently evinced those characteristics that have historically been branded as middlebrow: the willful mixture of entertainment and art, the profane and the sacred, frivolous and profound, erotic and intellectual. Even with the consecration of what used to be called the avant-garde and the invasion of former bastions of high culture by a proliferation of new media, the Broadway musical continues to epitomize a middle-class, middlebrow form beloved of suburbanites and tourists.

The categorization of musical theater as a middlebrow art is unquestionably related to the fact that it was long ignored or derided by university theater and music departments. To all but legions of enthusiastic theatergoers, musicals were considered, in Gerald Mast's pithy account, "essentially frivolous and silly diversions: lousy drama and lousy music."[16] By way of example, in a comprehensive, 780-page book on modernist theater, *Century of Innovation* (1973), historians Oscar Brockett and Robert Findlay devote a mere two paragraphs to the musical, despite their concession that it represents "the most popular form" of theater.[17] For many theater scholars and musicologists, the musical is embarrassingly commercial and too closely linked to high school drama clubs—as well as gay and lesbian subcultures. Indeed, the intense pleasure it arouses in its aficionados militates against it, in effect decreeing that it is too much fun to be worthy of academic study. I would argue, to the contrary, that its dubious legitimacy, its intermediary position between highbrow and lowbrow, is in fact symptomatic of its privileged status as a barometer of cultural and social politics.

MIDDLEBROW DISTINCTION

As an illustration of the musical theater's uncomfortable position in U.S. culture, let me consider the correlation between the Broadway musical and the Pulitzer Prize, an award that has functioned historically to define upper-middlebrow excellence. When the prize for drama was first given in 1918, it was explicitly charged with uplifting a stage that was then dominated by musical comedy, melodrama, and farce. Indeed, the drama award was the only one in the arts to mandate that the winning text should instill "educational value and power" and so improve the genre in question, "raising the standard of good morals, good taste, and good manners."[18] The clause about "raising the standard" was dropped from the description in 1929 thanks to the work of Eugene O'Neill and his contemporaries in institutionalizing a serious American theater. But the "'uplift' clause" remained on the books until 1964 (Hohenberg, 102 and 266–69).

Given the Pulitzer Prize guidelines, musicals have comprised a contentious category, in part because the mixture of highbrow and lowbrow is more visible and, for some, unsettling, in them than in other dramatic genres. Only eight pieces of musical theater have won the award, roughly one per decade beginning in the 1930s: *Of Thee I Sing* (1931), *South Pacific* (1949), *Fiorello!* (1959), *How to Succeed in Business Without Really Trying* (1961), *A Chorus Line* (1975), *Sunday in the Park with George* (1984), *Rent* (1996), *Next to Normal* (2010), and *Hamilton* (2015). Given the history of critical discomfort, it is little wonder that musicals have accounted for less than 10% of the awards. When the jury honored the Gershwins' *Of Thee I Sing*, it felt obliged to adopt a defensive posture: "This award may seem unusual, but the play is unusual. Not only is it coherent and well-knit enough to class as a play, aside from the music, but it is a biting and true satire on American politics." It is telling that although the librettists and lyricist were singled out, George Gershwin was ignored in the citation despite the fact that his score borrows liberally, if satirically, from the conventions of operetta and opera. But the music was deemed an "aside" that made the work distinctive but did not contribute substantially to its "admirable" qualities.[19] While most critics applauded the selection, Brooks Atkinson, the long-reigning drama critic of the *New York Times* (historically the most powerful proponent of upper-middlebrow taste) excoriated the committee for "turn[ing] its back on the drama" and for having stripped the prize of "a great deal of its value" (quoted in Toohey, 102).

Among the eight musicals, I want to look briefly at the cultural positioning of two, *South Pacific* and *Rent*.[20] The former is emblematic of the formally and politically ambitious musicals of the postwar years, the latter of a theater forced by changes in popular music, social mores, and conceptions of personal identity to loosen the postwar formulas. The former is the only Rodgers and Hammerstein musical to be awarded the Pulitzer Prize and remains, in Stanley Green's estimation, their "most universally admired achievement."[21] The latter, meanwhile, succeeded in reviving both the American musical and the rock opera at a time when both had been left for dead. Its critical acclaim and great popularity (especially with younger audiences) mark it as a telling index of a society in which cultural hierarchies have been all but overturned and abjection has been increasingly commercialized. Both plays are war stories that feature the death of a protagonist, one pitting its heroes against the Japanese, the other against poverty, exploitation, heroin, and AIDS. Both feature cross-race romances in which persons of color are exoticized and sexualized. Both oppose what is supposed to be an indigenous, authentic folk culture to American commercialism. Both were sensationally successful in appealing to politically liberal, middle-class audiences, chalking up long Broadway runs and spinning off popular recordings and movies. And both plays recycle musical and dramatic tropes associated with opera, combine them with the pop vernaculars of their day, and in part are precisely about that mixing. *Rent* suggests that despite the breakdown of the mid-century cultural hierarchy and an unprecedented diversification of media, the Broadway musical remains stuck in a middlebrow groove.

Rodgers and Hammerstein's fourth stage musical, *South Pacific* had the largest advance sale of any Broadway musical up to its time. Not only were Rodgers and Hammerstein the leading brand name in the Broadway musical by 1949, but the musical's source, James Michener's *Tales of the South Pacific*, had also the year before won the Pulitzer Prize for fiction. So no one was surprised when the musical garnered almost unanimous rave reviews, became "the 'hottest' ticket that Broadway had ever known," and went on to become the then-second longest running musical, surpassed only by *Oklahoma!* (Toohey, 237).

Although only implied in most reviews, critics seemed especially impressed by the writers' "courage" in making "the secondary love plot . . . a plea for racial tolerance," complete with a song ("You've Got to Be Carefully Taught") that, according to one commentator, "attacks the issue with a vehemence never before . . . seen on the stage."[22] And while the contradiction between an explicitly antiracist politics (one year after Truman desegregated the military) with the racist exoticization of the South Seas natives has made many people uncomfortable, *South Pacific* is celebrated in most critical accounts of musical theater as a "cherished legend" that, in Philip Beidler's words, makes "a courageous statement against racial bigotry in general and institutional racism in the postwar United States in particular."[23] Although this mythology vastly oversimplifies and whitewashes the musical's racial politics, it is also responsible for reconstructing *South Pacific* as a middlebrow masterpiece: a politicized, hence morally uplifting, example of a frivolous theatrical form designed to appeal to liberal fractions of the middle and upper-middle classes.

Although hailed as Rodgers and Hammerstein's most accomplished *Gesamtkunstwerk*, *South Pacific* is in fact a perfect illustration of the sleight of hand responsible for producing the illusion of the so-called integrated musical—for none of their other works is as much the jerrybuilt collage that *South Pacific* is. Beidler's list of its components ranges neatly from highbrow to lowbrow: the "grandeur of opera; the seriousness of 'legitimate' theatre; the comedic possibilities of the variety show and vaudeville; the emotionality of melodrama" (Beidler, 214–15). And it is hardly coincidental that the hero, Emile de Becque, happens to be French (although played originally by Ezio Pinza, a leading Italian basso), since the score is suffused by a French-inspired orientalism that gives it much of its highbrow appeal, including its echoes of the orientalist operas of Delibes and Saint-Saëns, the modernist exoticism of Debussy and Ravel, and the sexualized yet innocent South Seas women popularized by Gauguin. Uncharacteristically for Rodgers and Hammerstein, however, the main plot is somewhat less highbrow in tone and structure than the subplot, despite its more Europeanized music. (In almost all their other musicals, a more vaudevillian subplot is subordinate in brow level.)[24] For while the main plot pits an American "hick," Nellie Forbush, against a cosmopolitan, rich European, the subplot could have come out of any number of nineteenth-century French operas that feature a white hero who ventures into a mysterious land filled with dark-skinned natives and succumbs to the seductions of a native temptress. And as in most every orientalist narrative, Western liberal, humanist values finally triumph over oriental despotism, despite—or perhaps because of—Lieutenant Cable's death. Sacrificed both to the American war effort and the then-unforgiving laws of cross-race desire, Cable can resolve an otherwise unresolvable plotline only by dying.

Like *South Pacific*, *Rent* aims to ennoble a popular form by making a political statement. Unlike the scrupulously plotted Rodgers and Hammerstein music drama, Jonathan Larson's multicultural rock opera is a deliberately disheveled affair. *Rent* takes pleasure in mixing musical, poetic, and dramatic styles and in bringing together all those persons that give social conservatives the heebee-jeebees: "faggots, lezzies, dykes, cross dressers," junkies, anarchists, the homeless, people with AIDS, and artists of all stripes.[25] Moreover, its translation of *La Bohème* into a "Lower East Side story" mixes high and low more aggressively than any other musical of the 1990s, turning the frail Mimi into an S/M-club stripper and junkie, the musician Schaunard into a transvestite who dies of AIDS, and "Musetta's Waltz" into a few feverish guitar licks. Unlike Puccini's opera, which does not take up explicitly political issues, Larson's first act ends with a celebration of "going against the grain," of "Revolution, . . . /Forcing changes, risk, and danger," of "Tear[ing] down the wall" (Larson, 1996, 1: 23).

Like *South Pacific* before it, *Rent* mixes elite and popular cultures, despite the fact that its appeal across generations and classes testifies to the deterioration of the cultural hierarchy that had been in place fifty years before. On the one hand, the piece appropriates the plot and characters of what continues to epitomize old-fashioned, high-culture: opera. On the other hand, it cops a hipper-than-thou attitude, recycling the forms, technologies, and conventions of new media and performance; taking up for its guiding philosophy a kind of pop existentialism ("There is no future/There is no past/I live this moment/As my last," 1: 15); and exploiting the chic of "anything taboo," particularly when it is embodied by a sexual avant-garde that comes in all colors and flavors (1:23). At the same time, *Rent* is unabashedly populist in its use of music best described as commercial, corporate rock with touches of rhythm and blues, house music, techno, and club. Unlike *South Pacific*, which borrows musical styles conscious of their histories and associations, *Rent* uses a more disorderly and at times arbitrary mélange of styles.

Rent's unique positioning in the cultural field and its proven appeal to white, middle-class adolescents and young adults lies in its claim to a kind of gritty authenticity. For the production team was especially anxious that *Rent* not be seen to exploit and commodify the experiences of persons who, by any measure, must be numbered among the abject. They were very nervous, for example, that the musical should present an "honest" picture of the homeless rather than an "insulting" "chorus of cute homeless people."[26] Michael Greif, the director, was particularly concerned that *Rent* maintain the balance that has long characterized middlebrow: "I think the issue has always been preserving authenticity . . . in the way we present these characters, and also presenting them in ways that make them very identifiable and sympathetic and human."[27] In order to make *Rent* a commercial property, Greif and the producers made several decisions. Although the cast of the first New York Theatre Workshop reading had been "nearly all-white," it became "increasingly racially diverse" as the play neared production (quoted in Larson, 1997, 35). Greif's singling out of Daphne Rubin-Vega for seeming "like she really lived in that world—not in the world of musical theater," betrays an assumption on the part of the production team that persons of color—who play five of the eight major roles—give the musical the aura of authenticity they so desperately wanted it to have. For like *South Pacific*, *Rent* uses persons of color to turn what would otherwise be just another Broadway commodity into "the real thing" (Michael Greif, quoted in Larson, 1997, 26). Unlike *South Pacific*, however, *Rent* completely sidesteps issues of racial discrimination, using its persons of color to provide an audience the *New York Times* describes as young, middle-class, and "not exactly rainbow-colored" with an exotic, multicultural experience guaranteed to make it feel liberal and hip.[28] Moreover, although it was written during a period when hip hop had become the most popular music form in the United States, *Rent* remains as white as *South Pacific* in its musical pedigree and, with the exception of Angel's house-music-inspired "Today 4 U," virtually ignores the unprecedented richness of both African American and Latino musical forms.

Although musicals continue to win Pulitzer Prizes in the twenty-first century, the Broadway demographic has altered considerably since the 1990s, due in part to very real changes in the production and consumption of live theatre in the new, cleaned-up, family-friendly Times Square. Surveys show that since the opening of *Rent* in 1996, the Broadway audience has become not only richer but also younger. The number of spectators under twenty-five has grown from

20.9% to 23.9 per cent, while the number between the ages of thirty-five and forty-nine has declined from 31.8% to 25.1%. At the same time, Broadway has become a major tourist destination, as the number of tourists both from the United States and abroad has skyrocketed from 47.2% to 64.5%.[29] Much of this growth is a result of the invasion of Broadway by Disney Theatricals, beginning with *Beauty and the Beast* in 1994. Since then, Disney has opened five other musicals, none of which, except perhaps Julie Taymor's *The Lion King*, aspires to the kind of upper-middlebrow prestige that the Pulitzer Prize rewards. In an age of hyper-consumerism, these musicals have significantly changed the economics of Broadway. For the Disney musical—like the other new genre, the jukebox musical—does not require star performers or directors. Indeed, star performers would be liabilities because they would distract attention from the true stars of the show, which are the intellectual properties. In the case of most of the Disney musicals or Dreamworks' *Shrek*, the point is the near reproduction of the cinematic original. With the notable exception of Taymor, stage directors aim to recreate an animated film onstage while actors are fired if they deviate from their cartoon doppelgangers. And a musical that does not require a Patti LuPone or Nathan Lane is far more economical for producers because they can pay Equity scale rather than $4,000 a week. (It is important to note here that Disney has the economic clout to have been able to negotiate a 6% lower pay scale with Equity than the League of American Theaters and Producers [$1,465 minimum versus $1,558]).[30] Consumers are willing to pay $125 a head because they know they are getting a consumer-tested and familiar brand—satisfaction guaranteed by Disney or Dreamworks. The star power that used to be associated with writers, actors, and directors has been displaced onto corporations, which are the true Broadway stars in the twenty-first century. They are the bestowers of identity, community, and the magical power of the franchise.

In contrast to the Disney musical, the jukebox musical finds its star in an absent singer/songwriter. Affluent tourists go to *Mamma Mia!* or *Jersey Boys* not for the leading actor or plot or mise en scène, but to see performed the now classic pop songs featured in the show. (Both Disney and jukebox musicals are more appealing to non-anglophone spectators than traditional book musicals because audiences are likely to know the films on which the Disney musicals are based and the songs featured in jukebox musicals.) Since *Buddy—The Buddy Holly Story* in 1990, about twenty jukebox musicals have opened on Broadway, from the wildly successful *Mamma Mia!* based on the music of ABBA (which has grossed over $360 million) to expensive flops like *Good Vibrations* (the Beach Boys) and *Ring of Fire* (Johnny Cash). In comparison with the success of the Disney formula, the jukebox musical has proven a more hit-or-miss affair. And it, too, is difficult to place generically because it represents a hybrid of a rock concert (an already theatricalized event) and a play that might or might not be based on the life of its subject. But in all cases, the allure of the jukebox musical is largely nostalgic—one goes to *Mamma Mia!* in part to dance in the aisles and so relive one's youth or indulge in a fantasy reconstruction of the 1970s. The power of nostalgia suggests to me that the jukebox musical produces a different kind of star: *you*—for it provides a certain narcissistic gratification by evoking memories of "Dancing Queen" or "Money, Money, Money" and in the process making your own past a part of the performance. Unlike the old-fashioned backstage musical, such as *Follies*, which is haunted by *its own* past, the jukebox musical is haunted by *yours*.

Despite the invasion of Broadway by multinational corporations and simulations of mass culture, musicals remain an archaic mode of production that seems almost embarrassingly quaint in a culture of hyper-marketing and instant celebrity. Moreover, because stage musicals are still handmade, even Disney and Dreamworks have been unable to replicate on Broadway the kind of mass distribution on which their Hollywood empires thrive. And until choruses, theater orchestras, and stagehands are replaced by robots or machines, the musical will remain the most labor-intensive of Broadway theater forms. Despite its archaic, handmade quality, however, it seems incapable of amassing the cultural cachet that other long-established art forms enjoy. The bourgeois consumers who flock to *Jersey Boys* and *Shrek* continue to unnerve the guardians of what remains of high culture despite these audiences' economic and educational capital (Broadway League and Hauser, 31 and 29). Lincoln Center Theatre may have produced a widely acclaimed revival of *South Pacific*, but even this most prestigious among New York theaters is eclipsed by ballet and opera companies, symphony orchestras, and art museums, which retain a more verifiably highbrow patina and are more adept at enticing the social and economic elite to their boards of directors. The cultural stratification enshrined in the 1949 *Life* magazine chart may have become infinitely more complex in the intervening years, but the Broadway musical, I believe, remains a problematic affair—neither popular nor esoteric, hip nor sophisticated, trivial nor consequential *enough*—condemned to a middlebrow purgatory.

NOTES

1. See Gabriel J. Adams, "A Quick History of the Phantom of the Opera," *Ezine Articles*, http://ezinearticles.com/?A-Quick-History-Of-The-Phantom-Of-The-Opera&id=689698, accessed May 23, 2008.

2. Bertolt Brecht, "Against Georg Lukács," in *Aesthetics and Politics*, ed. Ronald Taylor (London: Verso, 1980), p. 83.

3. Broadway League and Karen Hauser, *The Demographics of the Broadway Audience, 2007–2008* (New York: Broadway League, 2008), pp. 31 and 29.

4. See Jack Poggi, *Theater in America: The Impact of Economic Forces, 1870–1967* (Ithaca, NY: Cornell University Press, 1968), p. 71.

5. See Richard Koszarski, *An Evening's Entertainment: The Age of the Silent Feature Picture 1915–1928* (Berkeley: University of California Press, 1990), p. 15.

6. Lawrence W. Levine, *Highbrow/Lowbrow: The Emergence of Cultural Hierarchy in America* (Cambridge, MA: Harvard University Press, 1988), pp. 221–22.

7. Thomas Herbert Dickinson, *The Insurgent Theatre* (New York: Benjamin Blom, 1972 [1917]), p. 83.

8. Richard Butsch, *The Making of American Audiences: From Stage to Television, 1750–1990* (Cambridge: Cambridge University Press, 2000), pp. 125 and 127.

9. Oliver Martin Sayler, *Our American Theatre* (New York: Brentano's, 1923), p. 247.

10. Walter Prichard Eaton, *The American Stage of To-Day* (Boston: Small, Maynard, 1908), p. 324; George Jean Nathan, *The Popular Theatre* (New York: Knopf, 1918, revised 1923), p. 81.

11. Janice Radway, "On the Gender of the Middlebrow Consumer and the Threat of the Culturally Fraudulent Female" (*South Atlantic Quarterly* 93:4 [Fall 1994]: 871–93), p. 872.

12. Janice Radway, "The Scandal of the Middlebrow: The Book-of-the-Month Club, Class Fracture, and Cultural Authority" (*South Atlantic Quarterly* 89:4 [Fall 1990]: 703–36), p. 733, n. 7.

13. Russell Lynes, "Highbrow, Lowbrow, Middlebrow," in *The Tastemakers* (New York: Harper & Brothers, 1954), p. 318.

14. Michael G. Kammen, *American Culture, American Tastes: Social Change and the 20th Century* (New York: Knopf, 1999), p. 96.

15. "High-brow, Low-brow, Middle-brow" (*Life* [April 11, 1949]: 100–101).

16. Gerald Mast, *Can't Help Singin': The American Musical on Stage and Screen* (Woodstock, NY: Overlook Press, 1987), p. 1.

17. Oscar G. Brockett and Robert R. Findlay, *Century of Innovation: A History of European and American Theatre and Drama since 1870* (Englewood Cliffs, NJ: Prentice-Hall, 1973), p. 567.

18. John Hohenberg, *The Pulitzer Prizes: A History of the Awards in Books, Drama, Music, and Journalism, Based on the Private Files over Six Decades* (New York: Columbia University Press, 1974), p. 19.

19. John L. Toohey, *A History of the Pulitzer Prize Plays* (New York: Citadel Press, 1967), p. 99.

20. For a more extensive analysis of these two musicals, see David Savran, "Middlebrow Anxiety," *A Queer Sort of Materialism: Recontextualizing American Theater* (Ann Arbor: University of Michigan Press, 2003), pp. 3–55.

21. Stanley Green, *The World of Musical Comedy* (New York: Da Capo, 1980), p. 216.

22. David Ewen, *Complete Book of the American Musical Theatre* (New York: Henry Holt, 1959), p. 265; Mark Kirkeby, liner notes to 1998 CD reissue of original cast recording of South Pacfic (Sony SK 60722), p. 9.

23. Philip D. Beidler, "South Pacific and American Remembering; or 'Gosh, We're Going to Buy This Son of a Bitch!'" (*Journal of American Studies* 27 [1993]: 207–22), p. 213.

24. Richard Rodgers writes: "If the main love story is serious, the secondary romance is usually employed to provide comic relief—such as Ado Annie and Will Parker in *Oklahoma!* or Carrie Pipperidge and Mr. Snow in *Carousel*. But in *South Pacific* we had two serious themes, with the second becoming a tragedy when young Cable is killed during the mission." Richard Rodgers, *Musical Stages: An Autobiography* (New York: Random House, 1975), p. 259.

25. Jonathan Larson, *Rent* libretto, Dreamworks compact discs DSMD2-50003, 1996, pp. 1: 23. Because there are no page numbers, I identify the source of lyrics by citing act and song number. All further references are noted in the text.

26. Michael Yearby and Jim Nicola, quoted in Larson, *Rent, with interviews and text by McDonnell and Silberger* (New York: William Morrow, 1997), pp. 40 and 23.

27. Quoted in Larson, *Rent, with interviews and text by McDonnell and Silberger* (New York: William Morrow, 1997), p. 25.

28. Weber, "Renewing the Lease on the Innocence of Youth" (*New York Times* [August 18, 2000]: E2).
29. Broadway League and Hauser, 20 and 10. These statistics cover the changes from the 1997–98 season to 2007–08.
30. See http://www.actorsequity.org/AboutEquity/contracts.asp, accessed March 15, 2009.

PART TWO

AUDIENCES

5

Box Office

STEVEN ADLER

■ □ ■

Money makes the world go around . . .
That clinking clanking sound
Can make the world go 'round!

FRED EBB KNEW WHEREOF HE wrote when he penned these lyrics for the film version of *Cabaret*, capturing not only the crass cynicism of the cabaret but also the hothouse environment of producing musical theater on Broadway.[1] Much as Times Square sits at the confluence of Broadway and Seventh Avenue, the production of musical theater resides at the intersection of art and commerce and is exemplified by the term "box office." Whether one subscribes to the *Oxford English Dictionary*'s claim that the term refers, historically, to the office that books box seats or to the notion that the cash-box resides there,[2] "box office" is the literal and figurative locus of the essential transaction between seller/producer and buyer/audience. The cramped little booths are supplemented now by cyber-Doppelgängers, but the term is still fraught with meaning on Broadway. It reverberates with Ebb's "clinking, clanking sound"—raising, spending, and making money. Box office connotes ticket sales, also known as "the gate," quantified in dollar figures as "the take" or "the gross." *Variety*, the bible of the entertainment industry, employs a playful lexicon of Runyonesque terms—"crix" (critics), "auds" (audiences), "helmers" (directors), "tuners" (musicals), and "legit" (the theater, as opposed to vaudeville or burlesque)—to capture the idiosyncratic spirit of film, television, and theater. One salient page of each issue reveals "Legit Grosses." This compendium of audience attendance and ticket sales provides a graphic representation of the changing fortunes of producing on Broadway.

For much of the twentieth century, producing musical theater was a profit-making enterprise wrought by solo entrepreneurs with a penchant for showmanship. The center of this activity was unequivocally Broadway. As the century waned, economic and artistic forces conspired to shift the nature of producing. Some institutional theaters in New York City and around the nation, once a bastion of the not-for-profit motive and offering an antidote to the perceived frivolity and pointlessness of Broadway, began to produce musicals with an eye toward burnishing their national reputations and sharing in the riches of the Great White Way.[3] On Broadway, raising money grew more challenging, and individual producers discovered that extensive partnerships, sometimes with the powerful real estate moguls who owned the theaters, provided the best means of mounting shows. Corporations, with extensive financial and marketing resources, recognized fertile territory in the hardscrabble terrain of midtown Manhattan and joined the fray. A Broadway presence might bolster the corporate brand, as with Disney, or enable exploitation of successful New York productions in corporate-controlled touring houses throughout the nation, as with Clear Channel.

Over the decades, the landscape changed dramatically, but through it all, "box office" has remained the sine qua non of producing. This chapter examines the critical link between money and art, and draws on new interviews with key players in the box-office arena—producers, attorneys, critics, general managers, and investors—providing valuable opportunities to look beyond the marquee and *Playbill* to evaluate how box office shapes the making of musicals.

ART AND COMMERCE

Jeffrey Seller (producer of the Tony Award–winning musicals *Rent, Avenue Q,* and *In the Heights*) offers his definition of box office with unhesitating precision:

> Box office is life and death. No matter how much we love the art form, we live and die according to how many people bought tickets yesterday at our box office. Life at a Broadway musical begins and ends at the box office. It begins the day you put it on sale and ends the day you close because you couldn't sell enough tickets. You have the sales, you're a winner; you don't have the sales, you're a loser, and that's all that matters. [4]

Paul Libin (producing director and vice president of Jujamcyn Theatres, which owns five Broadway theaters and frequently co-produces both musicals and straight plays) elaborates:

> In the last century, when a Broadway show opened and was praised with rave reviews from the critics, a long line of ticket-buyers at the theater quickly confirmed that the show was "box office." The meaning of "box office" is the unique collaboration of a playwright or composer, lyricist, book writer, director, cast of actors, designers, and many others. Theatergoers come to see the show, it triggers exuberant word of mouth, and suddenly it's difficult to buy tickets—that's "box office." Nowadays, you have to have the same response, although theatergoers line up via their computers and telephones. The show still means "box office." [5]

He notes, in illustration, the particularly remarkable day after *The Producers* opened in 2001 at Jujamcyn's St. James Theatre:

> After the rave reviews came out, we had a line going all the way down 44th Street around Broadway, almost around the corner. I called the Shuberts.[6] I asked them if we could implement the computer system at their Majestic and Broadhurst theater box offices to take some ticket-buyers off our long line so we could relieve the pressure at the St. James box office. That, to me, is the essence of what box office is about. It's not that you go to a window to buy the ticket, but that there are long lines of theatergoers buying the ticket. That day we sold $3,029,179 worth of tickets to *The Producers,* a Broadway record to date.

The exuberant praise critics heaped upon *The Producers* helped propel the musical to a fiscally rewarding six-year run. But critics can also be parsimonious in their response, negatively affecting sales and precipitating a show's quick and humiliating demise. Box-office success is essential for the health and longevity of a Broadway musical.

To acknowledge that "box office" refers to the Rube Goldberg–like mechanism by which producers finance and market shows is to accept Libin's assertion that this complex commercial transaction links inextricably to the artistic development of a production. From *Show Boat* in 1927 (possible because of impresario Florenz Ziegfeld's belief that Kern and Hammerstein could deliver a blockbuster) to *The Little Mermaid* in 2008 (possible because Disney Theatrical exists primarily to reinforce the corporate brand), the production of professional musical theater presents a tantalizing opportunity to examine the cohabitation of art and commerce.

RISKS AND REWARDS

Until the 1940s, Broadway musicals were most often aimed at audiences seeking diversion in a bright score, romance, comedy, dancing, and perhaps a touch of scandal and sex. Producers, then as now, attempted to discover the alchemical formula that might ensure a hit and tried to repeat successes whenever possible; inevitably, there was much reinvention and rarely innovation. And today's theatergoers remain averse to paying hefty Broadway ticket prices for risky material; safe, tried, and true shows are more attractive to audiences and more lucrative for producers and investors. Much of what seems like the radically new on Broadway first saw life in a previous incarnation. Frank Rich, the *New York Times* lead drama critic from 1980 to 1994, explains:

> The entire history of the Broadway musical is that people see a hit and try to imitate it. Then comes a period when those imitations are successful and attract more backers until the cycle passes, as it always does in show business. *My Fair Lady* brought in an epidemic of British or ersatz British musicals often set in period. *Cats* brought in the spectacle. *Rent* is a direct antecedent of several shows running now, like *Passing Strange* and *Spring Awakening*. It is what always happens in show business and not just in the Broadway musical. Someone sees something that works and money follows it because it is still a marketplace. After *Les Misérables*, we still have epic adaptations of classics, or pseudo-classics, with huge special effects. That has always been the way. The number of dollars may change. But *Hairspray* is a hit, so every John Waters movie or movie like a John Waters movie is turned upside down to be a musical. *Hairspray* has surely launched *The Wedding Singer*, *Legally Blonde*, and *Cry-Baby*.[7]

In Broadway's early years, new productions competed annually for available theater space, and very few shows ran for more than a year or two. According to *Variety*, in the decades prior to 1943, when *Oklahoma!* made its mark as the first truly integrated book musical, only two musicals ran more than 1,000 performances[8]—the Depression-era musical revues *Pins and Needles* and *Hellzapoppin.*[9] No book musical experienced such success, and few plays survived that long. However, musicals rarely needed to run very long to make a profit. Although ticket prices were much less expensive than today, when adjusted for inflation, production costs were proportionally lower than now, and a modest run could reap a tidy profit. Today, long runs are necessary if producers hope to recoup a production's investments and pay a profit.

Long runs, although usually profitable, present challenges. Seth Gelblum, a leading theater and entertainment attorney, observes that there were more theaters on Broadway in the first half of the twentieth century than at the start of the twenty-first:

> Today you can't mount that many shows a year; you can't easily raise that much money, and you can't find the space for the shows. Since shows started running for long periods of time—a phenomenon of the last twenty years—it has put a terrible pinch on theater availability. As a result, producers can't produce a new musical every year like some of the great producers did. They can't find a space and they're out raising money all the time. As a result, it's not a job anymore. It's an occasional killing, if it works.[10]

Producers evaluate a theater's location, stage size, sightlines, ambience, and seating capacity to determine where to house a production. When fewer theaters are available, musicals stack up like planes in a holding pattern, often circling for years to land at the right venue.

For much of the twentieth century, producing was a relatively lonely enterprise. Individual producers or small partnerships oversaw every aspect of the production process: identifying the property; luring backers, or "angels," who might share opinions with the producer but had no contractual artistic or managerial oversight; hiring the artistic team; and serving as arbiters of every element in the show. Today, the costs of producing a new musical render the solo producer an antiquated relic. Even Cameron Mackintosh, producer of many spectacularly staged British imports that populated Broadway in the 1980s, collaborated when necessity demanded, most recently with Disney Theatrical on *Mary Poppins*.

FROM "ANGELS" TO "INVESTORS"

The names above the title in a contemporary Broadway musical's *Playbill* reveal the complex fiscal, personal, and artistic relationships that producers nurture in order to bring a musical to the stage. *Spring Awakening* received bountiful critical praise and eight Tony Awards in 2007. Modestly staged with a small orchestra and a cast of twenty young actors, it suffers nothing by the absence of impressive scenic effects or lavish costumes and was relatively inexpensive in comparison to larger-cast and more opulent musicals, costing, according to its general manager, Abbie Strassler, roughly $6 million.[11] (Lavish productions can cost $20 million or more.) Yet *Spring Awakening*'s producing credits speak eloquently to the necessity for producers to cultivate large investor networks to nurture a musical over several years through various incarnations. Its evolutionary path involved readings and workshops at La Jolla Playhouse, Sundance Institute's Summer Theatre Laboratory, Roundabout Theatre Company, and Lincoln Center, and a not-for-profit Off Broadway staging at the Atlantic Theatre

Company, before it opened on Broadway. Each of those productions incurred expenses. Twenty-seven individual and partnership names appear above the title of *Spring Awakening*, most of them investors whose contributions earned them the cachet of a producing credit, although they enjoyed no artistic oversight. Attorney Seth Gelblum notes,

> *Spring Awakening* was a very risky thing to do, and as a result, it was hard to find people willing to write huge checks, so they had to go to more people. When it's a riskier show like that—a dark, "downtown" show—it takes more and more people, so the numerical threshold with respect to how much you have to invest to get your name above the title goes down. It's easier to get your name above the title on a show where they need the money.

The trend in billing inflation trumpets the ascendancy of the investor in a marketplace in which it grows increasingly difficult to capitalize productions. Jeffrey Seller and Kevin McCollum produced two of the more durable musicals around the turn of the twenty-first century, *Rent* and *Avenue Q*, as well as the 2008 Tony-winning *In the Heights*. Seller contrasts their approach with that of the producers of *Spring Awakening*:

> There is no such billing on *Rent* or *Avenue Q*, and although we have seven entities over the title of *In the Heights*, it is modest by today's standards. Kevin and I have been blessed with the ability to produce as we wish to produce and what we wish to produce, under terms that are very rewarding and satisfying to us. That is due in large measure to our first success with *Rent* and the type of material we choose to produce. Kevin and I have made our living solely in the theater. We are certainly a rare beast on Broadway now; there are perhaps ten producers who also make their living solely from the theater. There have always been people endowed with money that they either had in their family or earned from other places, who like to play on Broadway. That has

been enriching to Broadway. When a billionaire produces *Grey Gardens*, and takes it from [Off-Broadway theater] Playwrights Horizons to Broadway, that's good for Broadway. [But] it doesn't happen to be who I am.

In contrast to *Spring Awakening*, most musicals from the so-called Golden Age (roughly 1940s to 1960s) were the apparent creations of only one or two producers, but like their contemporaries, they were dependent upon investors. The wisdom that guides producing on Broadway is the more expensive the production, the longer it takes to pay back (recoup) the initial investment (capitalization). Investors do not earn a profit until the producer reimburses them for capitalization, which funds the development of the production through opening night. After opening, the production must survive on its weekly box-office gross, from which producers pay operating expenses such as salaries, royalties, theater rent, advertising, and equipment rental. If the gross receipts exceed the expenses—a large-scale, sold-out musical can earn more than $1 million a week but can cost more than $500,000 to run—producers distribute remaining funds to investors to pay back the capitalization. After a successful production recoups, producers and investors share any profits above weekly operating expenses. Producers forecast recoupment times based on projections of potential weekly box office. It can be difficult to attract investors if the recoupment time is long and the property risky.

Historically, about one of every five Broadway productions recoups its initial investment, a daunting statistic for a producer or investor. Broadway has never been a hospitable arena for speculators. The fanciful term "angel," once common parlance on Broadway, has yielded to the more prosaic but literal "investor." The evolution of terminology reflects a similar evolution in the landscape. Producing Broadway musicals is considerably more expensive in the twenty-first century than in the Golden Age. In 1943, *Oklahoma!*, which employed over fifty actors, cost roughly $100,000. Adjusted for inflation, this would equal about $1.25 million in 2008. If *Oklahoma!* were staged today, using contemporary stagecraft and a fifty-actor cast, it would cost close to $20 million—one reason that most revivals feature smaller casts than the original productions. Producers must consider theater rents, union-negotiated salaries, royalties, equipment, advertising, insurance, utilities, and development expenses for earlier versions of the show, as well as weekly operating expenses, when considering whether to proceed with a production.

Muscular box-office receipts and small capitalization result in rapid recoupment. *Rent*, according to producer Jeffrey Seller, recouped in about fifteen weeks because it was a hit of remarkable proportions. *Avenue Q*, another critical and box-office success, recouped in about forty weeks. However, as Seller notes, these were relatively inexpensive shows to produce. His more opulent production of Baz Luhrmann's 2002 *La Bohème* was initially budgeted at $6.5 million and eventually cost about $9 million. Seller observes, "That was not responsible producing—but nevertheless we got back the whole $2.5 million overage, and we got back another half-million dollars. The rest of it [$6 million] we lost."

Roy Furman has had a hand in producing on Broadway since 1974, participating as investor and producer on *Parade, Sweet Smell of Success, Dirty Rotten Scoundrels, Spamalot, The Color Purple,* and the 2008 revival of *Gypsy*. Before he considers involvement with a production, he asks essential questions: "Who is going to see this? Does it have an audience? Will that audience pay one hundred [dollars] or more a ticket? Who is doing it— the creative side and the producing side? The right producers mean a great deal."[12] While a producer or investor might be inclined to assess a production's prospects only through the lens of sound financial strategy, Furman noted that there are moments "when there's a rationale that transcends economics. That is, this show is art and art deserves to be produced. I've done a few of those, where I'll make the judgment that this has to be seen, it must be done, and in that instance I'm willing to put my money on the line to make it happen." He cited the 2008 *Gypsy* as an example. Five years earlier, Bernadette Peters had appeared in a revival of the Styne-Sondheim-Laurents classic. It was too soon, said many, for another production. However, Furman thought highly of the 2007 staged-concert version of the show at City Center's *Encores!* series and concluded that a wider audience deserved to see it. "This made [the producers] think sometimes that willingness, that conviction, emboldens everyone to move forward. It was an instance where I thought the audience had to see this performance and production." Furman's passion, intuition, and willingness to fund a considerable portion of the capitalization helped mount a production that garnered critical accolades and a healthy box office. This *Gypsy* dazzled not only because of Patti LuPone's heralded star turn as Rose but also because the producers concluded that the score would suffer if not performed by a full-sized, albeit costly, Broadway orchestra. To reduce costs, producers of revivals of musicals orchestrated originally for acoustic instruments rely more frequently on smaller orchestras complemented by synthesizers. In this instance, the producers' willingness—unusual on Broadway now—to hire twenty-five musicians signaled their belief in the vitality of the score, which in turn contributed to the power of the production.

RISK MANAGEMENT, AND A NEW ROLE FOR NOT-FOR-PROFIT THEATERS

In 2008, San Diego-based investment banker Ralph Bryan chaired the board of trustees of La Jolla Playhouse, a not-for-profit institutional theater that, in partnership with commercial producers, launched several musicals that later enjoyed successful commercial Broadway runs. Bryan invested in a number of Broadway musicals, including *Jersey Boys,* a box-office success that premiered at La Jolla and recouped on Broadway after only eight months. According to Bryan,

> Anyone who invests in a commercial production with the idea that they're *going* to make a lot of money has the wrong focus. However, everyone does it because there is the *chance* to make a significant amount of money. It is binary; you either lose it all or do very well. There is rarely a solid return. If you're doing a straight play with a star in a limited run, you have a chance of getting your money back and maybe some return beyond that. In a musical, you take that all-or-none risk for the huge upside. [*laughing*] It would be fun to make money more often than you lose it. [13]

Max Bialystock, the down-on-his-luck producer *cum* con artist at the center of the Mel Brooks musical *The Producers,* cautions his protégé Leo Bloom that there are two ground rules for producing: "One: never put your own money in the show, [and, two]: never put your own money in the show!" For much of the twentieth century, many successful producers rarely invested their own money, offering instead their taste, skill, and experience as collateral against the angels' investment. Some of them, like George Abbott, Richard Rodgers and Oscar Hammerstein II, and Harold Prince were theatrical artists in their own right, with exceptional insight into the process of making theater. Now, it is rare for an artist to produce; the skill sets have grown more divergent and specialized. In today's fiscal climate, producers tend to invest in their own shows in order to demonstrate good faith to potential backers. Jeffrey Seller notes,

I believe in putting my own money in shows; not so much that I'm going to have to sell my house if I fail, but I believe that a producer is showing confidence to the investors. . . . Today, most big producers are putting their own money into shows. I can't say they're putting in a million dollars or 10 percent of the budget, but I do think they're putting in hundreds of thousands.

Ralph Bryan adds the investor's perspective. "It's probably easier to commit when you think the producer has skin in the game, but I don't know ultimately if it affects the success ratio. No matter how hard you try, only one in four or five shows recoups."

Although the great producers of the Golden Age relied on angels, they maintained a profile of individuality and idiosyncratic leadership that contemporary producers infrequently display. They were, to varying degrees, artistic and fiscal risk-takers. Today, the magnitude of production costs has shaped a landscape increasingly hospitable to wealthy corporations and consortiums, which, Frank Rich notes, are rarely inclined to take risks. "*The Lion King* may be daring by Disney standards, but it's hardly a bold risk. It was based on one of the best-selling movie musicals on the planet and it was a spectacle." Alan Levey, former senior vice president of Disney Theatrical, explains, "Corporations will always be more interested in producing franchise titles to take advantage of the built-in awareness."[14] Rich ventures that many of the innovative musicals on Broadway first saw light in not-for-profit productions:

No Broadway producer in the mid-1970s would have originated *A Chorus Line*, and I doubt any Broadway producer now would have originated *Spring Awakening* or *Passing Strange* [all three shows transferred from Off-Broadway, not-for-profit theaters]. It still takes certain guts to take risks, and producers often fail to put their money on something risky, even if it has gotten acclaim in a non-profit venue. The day of the producer with highfalutin' tastes seems to be over.

Production costs inhibit risk-taking because "things are decided by committee." As Paul Libin observes,

> One of the problems confronting the theater nowadays is that there are producers making decisions who may not have the experience or the expertise in the theater. These persons make choices that are costly, or are unable to negotiate reasonable contracts. The way shows are currently financed requires many people investing large sums of money. Hopefully, those producers are strong enough and smart enough to make the decisions both artfully and economically that are going to enhance the production.

Frank Rich contends that very few producers now conceive new musicals the way that David Merrick, the formidable and swaggering power behind many hits of the 1950s and '60s, did with the original 1959 production of *Gypsy*. Merrick was a larger-than-life mogul who famously browbeat and blustered his way to blockbuster productions like *Gypsy, Hello, Dolly,!* and *42nd Street*. Although a lawyer by training, he insinuated himself into every aspect of his productions, from writing and design to marketing and advertising.[15]

Jeffrey Seller draws some critical distinctions about producing styles:

> It is what I call the difference between top-down or bottom-up producing. Is this an idea generated by a producer who said, "I think this will sell tickets," or is this an idea generated by an author who comes to a producer and says, "I need help

with this because I have a burning desire to do it"? There are top-down enterprises that have worked over the years. *Hello, Dolly!*, was David Merrick's idea. Cameron Mackintosh said to me that he had never done a show that was his idea. He does shows that artists bring to him. I took it to heart because none of the three shows that I produced that won Tonys for best musical was my idea in the least. They were shows that needed nurturing. Kevin [McCollum] and I got involved with them from the ground up and we helped them along, but their genius came from their authors. I believe history proves that this has been a better formula, but there are exceptions. Frequently, when a producer hires a writer to make a show, [the writer] doesn't bring to it that life because they did it for many reasons, some of which we know are financial. But it just doesn't burn with that kind of passion.

Seller and McCollum shepherded *Rent* from downtown workshop to resounding Broadway success. He and McCollum introduced the *Avenue Q* composer-lyricist team of Robert Lopez and Jeff Marx to librettist Jeff Whitty and director Jason Moore at a time when "the boys had only six songs and some sketch material." Harold Prince made a mark employing both methodologies. Director-choreographer Jerome Robbins conceived *West Side Story* and developed it with Arthur Laurents, Leonard Bernstein, and Stephen Sondheim. Prince and partner Robert Griffith agreed to produce the show only when others dropped or passed on the property. However, Prince, as producer and director, generated the initial vision of *Cabaret* and engaged John Kander, Fred Ebb, and Joe Masteroff to write it.

In the Golden Age, producers rarely dared to open "cold" on Broadway with a new show; instead, they tried out musicals in cities close to New York, like New Haven, Boston, and Philadelphia, before plunging into the turbulent waters of

Broadway. Now, musicals endure a longer process of development before they see the lights of Times Square. Few contemporary producers choose an out-of-town tryout due to the costs of mounting a show and then transporting it to another city. A typical approach now involves some combination of readings, workshops, and a less expensive, not-for-profit production before Broadway. This involves more time and planning than the older method and often extends the developmental period by several years. It also allows the creative team substantial time to refine the work, which was frequently impossible in rushed, out-of-town tryouts—*Spring Awakening*, for example, benefited greatly from multiple incarnations over a long gestation period. It is not without expense, however: a full-scale production at a not-for-profit regional theater, like La Jolla Playhouse or the Old Globe Theatre, can cost a commercial producer as much as $3 million in "enhancement money" in addition to several hundred thousand dollars from the institutional theater's budget.[16]

REDEFINING THE RELATIONSHIP BETWEEN ART AND COMMERCE

The relationship between commercial producers and not-for-profit theaters is a relatively new but vitally important factor. In strictly financial terms, commercial producers seek to earn profits for themselves and their investors; not-for-profit theaters return profits to the institutional coffers. The Public Theatre in New York City produced *A Chorus Line* and then transferred it to Broadway in 1975 without commercial involvement; the Public benefited from all profits. This musical, as groundbreaking for its developmental process as for its form and content, signaled to commercial producers that there was an attractive alternative to grooming a show for Broadway out of town. They sought less expensive, more hospitable venues in which to develop productions beyond the glare of the New York spotlight. Frank Rich highlights the difference between institutional theaters that serve as a testing ground for new musicals brought by commercial producers and institutional theaters that commission and create new work, citing artistic directors like Joseph Papp and George Wolfe of the Public Theatre and André Bishop of Lincoln Center as exemplars "who will take a chance using non-profit money and hope that someone will move it—or they'll move it themselves if it takes off." An institutional theater on Broadway, like Lincoln Center or the Roundabout, can run a successful musical indefinitely without transferring it to a commercial theater. This provides essential income, a necessity in the fiscally challenging world of producing not-for-profit theater. In most instances, commercial producers court institutional theaters, which recognize that there is much to gain from such a relationship. Steven A. Libman, former managing director of La Jolla Playhouse, acknowledges,

> We are devoted to the musical as a uniquely American art form and, therefore, we have a long history with musicals. We produce them primarily because they are artistically very important and, secondarily, because they generate a significant amount of revenue and allow us to grow our subscription base. We lose money on everything we do, but we lose less on a musical. We will lose less on a multi-million dollar, enhanced musical compared with a $500,000 straight show. Depending upon how long we run a musical, we can gross between $500,000 and $1 million in single-ticket sales alone, and I can convert a lot of those single-ticket buyers to subscribers.[17]

In the Golden Age, a commercial producer rolled the dice on an out-of-town tryout. Many productions closed in New Haven or Boston before ever playing Broadway, losing all of their capitalization. The commercial producer today will more willingly risk $2 million in enhancement money for an institutional production that may never transfer to Broadway, than $10 million to mount a commercial production that may flop out of town.

The potential risks for institutional theaters are more frequently organizational than fiscal. As Libman notes,

> You have to be very careful about how involved the outside producers get in the process of creating an enhanced musical or enhanced play. We are a non-profit and cannot be perceived as having the producers in the rehearsal studios telling the director what to do. We run the risk of adversely affecting our agreements with the unions. You have to be able to say to the producers, "You can attend some of the rehearsals but you can't attend all of them, and you really have to be invisible." The outside producers need to know that La Jolla Playhouse is in charge of *producing* the play, and has final say on all artistic matters.

Another threat is the strain that new musicals, because of their size and complexity, can impose. As Libman relates,

> They suck up more time. Our payroll can grow to an additional one hundred part-time employees. The new technology that we use is fascinating but expensive. Rehearsals take longer. You spend more money because you are doing a show where the potential single ticket income is at least $500,000, compared to up to $100,000 for a straight play. We have to constantly remind each other that we have other shows running at the same time so that the other show doesn't become the bastard stepchild of the large, enhanced musical.

The partnership of commercial and not-for-profit arenas was unthinkable a few decades earlier because of the perception of conflicting artistic and financial principles. Today, it offers a popular means of birthing new musicals. As Libman observes,

> In a sense, we have one foot in the non-profit world, but we're also part of the commercial theater world and the enhancement revenue that comes with it is significant. Sometimes, that makes it easier for us to say, "We can balance our budget if we do a big musical that's enhanced as opposed to a non-enhanced play." However, we always have to be careful and make sure the musical fulfills the mission of the organization. But it's like heroin, that enhancement money. It's wonderful for cash flow.

If successful on Broadway, the musical can return 1 to 2% of the gross to the institutional theater—perhaps $20,000 a week on a hit show

Regardless of the means of development, according to Alan Levey, "It all comes back to the story-telling. Without a good story, you have nothing." Good ideas may succeed in one venue but fail in another. Many new musicals that earn enthusiastic critical and audience reaction elsewhere fail on Broadway, where different expectations and audience demographics create a more challenging environment. In 2007, *A Catered Affair* was heralded at the Old Globe Theatre but lasted only three months on Broadway.

Producing wisdom, composed of equal parts experience and intuition, is essential in determining the future of new work. *Spring Awakening* played at the Off Broadway, not-for-profit Atlantic Theatre Company in spring 2006. Off Broadway, a designation that applies to a range of not-for-profit and commercial theaters throughout Manhattan, is a less expensive—and, with a maximum of 499 seats, less remunerative—venue than Broadway, where theaters can seat as many as 2,000. General manager Abbie Strassler explains the next steps in the producers' process:

When the producers saw they had such good reviews, they started thinking, "Should we do it Off-Broadway [in a commercial venue] or on Broadway?" We started running numbers and it just didn't make sense to raise money for a production of that size Off-Broadway. It's very difficult to raise money for Off-Broadway, because [in the investors' view] there's nothing sexy about Off-Broadway. At the time, there were fifteen actors and four musicians, and that's a lot for Off-Broadway. When I started running numbers for Broadway, it did make a little more sense, but I thought, "Oh my God, there's teenage sex, nudity, the word "fucked"! Most "legit" money people said, "You're out of your mind." We were taking a crapshoot. But there was so much passion between [lead producers] Ira Pittelman and Tom Hulce for the piece itself. The feeling was that we might lose some money, but it was worth it. It's groundbreaking and we had to do it.

Musical theater is the mainstay of Broadway's box office. In 2007–08, Broadway grossed $938 million, a robust figure that would have been higher if not for a nineteen-day stagehands' strike. Musicals accounted for approximately $820 million of the box office.[18] Moreover, Broadway and New York City enjoy a symbiotic fiscal relationship. During the city's economic downturn of the 1970s and early 1980s, many theaters were dark because producers lacked capital, and audiences were reluctant to venture into a blighted Times Square. Theater owners began to co-produce in order to populate their houses and generate income. The difficulty that producers encountered in raising money opened the doors to the so-called British Invasion of lavishly staged productions such as *Evita, Cats, Les Misérables, Starlight Express, The Phantom of the Opera,* and *Miss Saigon.* Many critics in the media and the theatrically sophisticated segment of the theatergoing audience bemoaned the state of the art and questioned whether the American musical would ever recover. The city's subsequent economic rebound occasioned the reinvigoration of musicals created in America. American-born hits like *Rent, Avenue Q, Hairspray, The Lion King, Jersey Boys, Spamalot,* and *Wicked,* playing in tandem with highly praised revivals of *Gypsy* and *South Pacific,* epitomize healthy Broadway box office at the beginning of this millennium. These productions reached Broadway by different paths and appeal to a wide cross-section of theatergoers. However, history teaches that the fiscal and artistic health of Broadway—once dubbed "the Fabulous Invalid"—is always unpredictable. Will escalating costs and ticket prices drive producers and audiences to the apparent safety of adaptations of mediocre movies and yet another iteration of *Grease,* or will innovation flourish with shows cut from the cloth of *Spring Awakening* and *Passing Strange*? Alan Levey, formerly of Disney, summed up the challenge. "Producers will have to become more creative, controlling the economic challenges faced by Broadway without stifling the creative process. Smart producing inspires creativity on both sides of the equation—the economics and the creative."

NOTES

1. Fred Ebb, lyrics for "Money, Money," music by John Kander, in *Cabaret,* dir. Bob Fosse, 1972.
2. *Oxford English Dictionary,* 2nd ed. (Oxford: Oxford University Press, 1989), www.oed.com/, accessed July 19, 2008.
3. Lincoln Center Theater, the Roundabout Theatre Company, and Manhattan Theatre Club are, as of this writing, not-for-profit theaters with Broadway houses whose productions are Tony-eligible. Second Stage may soon join their ranks.
4. Jeffrey Seller, telephone interview with the author, July 24, 2008.

5. Paul Libin, telephone interview with the author, July 23, 2008.

6. Author's note: the Shubert, Nederlander, and Jujamcyn organizations own or control thirty-one Broadway theaters.

7. Frank Rich, telephone interview with the author, July 3, 2008.

8. At eight performances a week, 1,000 performances amount to a run of slightly under two-and-a-half years, although some shows in the early twentieth century closed for the summer because theaters lacked air conditioning.

9. "Broadway Long Runs" (Chart in *Variety* [June 9–15, 2008]: 50).

10. Seth Gelblum, telephone interview with the author, June 27, 2008. An old Broadway maxim, attributed to playwright Robert Anderson, goes: "You can't make a living on Broadway, but you can make a killing."

11. Abbie Strassler, telephone interview with the author, July 15, 2008.

12. Roy Furman, telephone interview with the author, July 17, 2008.

13. Ralph Bryan, telephone interview with the author, June 30, 2008.

14. Alan Levey, telephone interview with the author, June 11, 2008.

15. See Howard Kissel's excellent 1993 biography, tellingly titled *David Merrick: The Abominable Showman* (New York: Applause Books, 1993).

16. Since the mid-1980s, two institutional theaters in San Diego, for example, La Jolla Playhouse and the Old Globe Theatre, have launched several Broadway productions. La Jolla Playhouse: *Big River, Dangerous Games, The Who's Tommy,*, the revival of *How to Succeed in Business Without Really Trying, Jane Eyre, Thoroughly Modern Millie, Dracula, the Musical, Jersey Boys, Cry-Baby,* and *Memphis.* Old Globe: *Into the Woods,* the revival of *Damn Yankees, Play On!, The Full Monty, Dirty Rotten Scoundrels, Dr. Seuss' How the Grinch Stole Christmas!, The Times They Are A-Changin',* and *A Catered Affair.*

17. Steven A. Libman., interview with the author, June 26, 2008.

18. The Broadway League, "Broadway Season Statistics at a Glance," www.broadwayleague.com/editor_files/Broadway%20 Statistics%20at%20a%20Glance.pdf, accessed August 2, 2008.

6

Audiences and Critics

MICHELLE DVOSKIN

■ □ ■

THE TERMS "AUDIENCE" AND "CRITIC" seem straightforward. The online *American Heritage Dictionary*'s first definition of audience is those "assembled at a performance. . . or attracted by a radio or television program." Thus, an audience comprises people who engage with a particular performance text—for example, musicals. "Critic" is similarly uncomplicated: "one who forms and expresses judgments," in this case, about musicals.[1] By these definitions, every audience member is also, fundamentally, a critic. Everyone who attends a musical, has a response to it, and then shares that response has acted the part of a critic, even if the response was as basic as applause (or lack thereof).

Of course, typically when we talk about musicals and critics, we refer to published critics, individuals who make their living experiencing and responding to musicals, alongside other forms of performance. These are most often writers with some knowledge about and interest in the form, and throughout the musical's history they have been influential in regard to both audiences' attitudes and size. While this specialized role continues to exist, more and more audience members are beginning to share it, thanks to the Internet and the self-publishing possibilities it offers.

While defining both terms and recognizing their relationship is easy on this basic level, thinking about how to make use of them as a scholar of musicals is more complicated. How do musicals affect audiences, and how do audiences affect musicals? How do we make use of and understand the work of critics, both professional and recreational? These are the questions I begin to address in this chapter.

AUDIENCES

In considering musicals' relationships to their audiences, we may begin by acknowledging two key things. The first is that musicals are an inherently commercial form. Audiences are crucial to their existence because musicals depend on ticket sales to survive. In commercial venues, the typical goal is to run for as long as possible, or more aptly, as long as sufficient seats are filled with paying customers. Even when musicals play in nonprofit venues, with limited runs, they are typically seen as ways to raise money for less commercially viable material in the season. This need to appeal to audiences affects the choices made by producers and creative teams, particularly as the cost of mounting a musical continues to grow rapidly. Historically, audiences directly influenced musicals' development via their responses during tryout performances. During musical theater's "Golden Age" (1943–approx. 1966), musicals were typically developed through out-of-town tryouts, when a new show played in other cities on its way to Broadway. Audience reaction served as feedback for the artistic team, who would then often make adjustments to the show to maximize its audience appeal. This dependence on popularity and responsiveness to audience appeal has tended to make people interested in "serious" theater view musicals with suspicion.[2]

The second key issue is the presence of musicals in a variety of media, since medium matters when thinking about reception practices. Musical *theater* is a live form, with performers sharing time and space with spectators. Like any live theater audience, musical theater audiences are part of a communal experience with other audience members as well as the performers and are "involved in a reciprocal relationship which can change the quality and success of a performance."[3] Most audiences are aware of their influence and manage their responses accordingly.

Movie musical audiences are also part of a group but one traditionally understood as more privatized. While watching other audience members at a live performance has historically been an expected part of the event, watching other spectators at a movie is much less common. There are other important differences as well. At a movie musical, the performers are not physically present; the filmic text will be the same every time, regardless of audience composition or response. The medium of film also allows a heightened level of control over reception. Through close-ups and other cinematic choices, film directors can ensure that their audience notices what they want them to, when they want them to. Theater directors, though they can use design and blocking to emphasize key moments or images, have much less control over the audience's gaze.

Television, a medium in which musicals are becoming increasingly popular, shares these elements of fixity and control with film. Television audiences, however, are generally understood as even more privatized than movie audiences. Most television is viewed in the home, either alone or with small groups of family and friends. This paradigm also holds true for film musicals released on DVD or video. Musicals that occur as part of episodic series, however, have a slightly different relationship to their audiences as a result of the fandom and familiarity built up over time. Many shows also have established fan communities, often online, which offer a designated, pre-existing place to share responses to the musical, if not the act of viewing itself.[4]

These differences affect how we think about audiences engaging with a given musical. Audiences watching *Chicago* on Broadway will have a different experience, and perform their responses differently, from audiences who saw the movie version in the theater, and their responses and performance will differ from those who watched it on DVD in their living rooms. For example, on Broadway one of the "merry murderesses" in "Cell Block Tango" might make eye contact with an audience member, who may then pay particular attention to her performances in group numbers. This kind of personalized connection isn't possible for a viewer of the filmed text. And while everyone who watches the movie version of *Chicago* will respond to the same text, audiences who see the live musical will see a different text each night, making generalizations about reception difficult even within a single production's run. One night, the actress playing Roxie Hart might be a little tired, lending a certain vulnerability to her characterization. Another night, a particularly exuberant audience might energize the whole company, creating entirely different nuances in the performances. And of course, in a long-running show like *Chicago*, cast members are frequently replaced. An audience member who saw Ann Reinking's Roxie responded to a different version of the character from one who saw Bianca Marroquin in the same role, in the same production, later in its run.

Despite these important differences, however, certain characteristics of musical reception tend to operate across media. One is the influence of cast albums, which extend aspects of the audience experience beyond the act of viewing the musical itself. Since *Oklahoma!* (1943), Broadway (and, increasingly, Off Broadway) musicals have typically recorded and marketed the original cast performing the songs, creating an often profitable artifact that can be purchased and enjoyed regardless of whether the listener has actually seen the production. Attachment to a cast album can follow from or precede attendance, and through this artifact, it becomes possible to understand oneself as a fan of a show without having seen it.[5] For those who do see a production, these albums grant some measure of permanence to the ephemeral medium of musical theater. While the actual experience of attending the show is impossible to replicate, cast albums allow audiences to relive their experience, offering not only the words and music but, in some measure, the performances of the singers.[6]

Although existing as artifacts themselves, movie musicals also typically release soundtracks that, like the album for a stage musical, allow audiences to engage in additional ways with the production in the space of their home. Even television musicals, which begin for audiences in the home, often take up this trend. For example, both *Xena: Warrior Princess* and *Buffy the Vampire Slayer* produced episodes framed as musicals, and each released a soundtrack. Joss Whedon, *Buffy's* executive producer and the writer/composer/lyricist of the musical episode, emphasized that the release of the album was as much about authenticating his episode as a "real musical" as it was about commerce. In his liner notes for the album, Whedon, a self-proclaimed musicals fan, made the association with authenticity clear: "Now I have a *real* soundtrack album of my musical. . . . This makes it *real*."[7]

If audio recordings, and the extended connection they allow, are a common thread across media, so also is the way in which audiences tend to experience musicals. Whether watching live performance, film, or television, audiences engage with musicals in particular ways, ways that have everything to do with the body. Increasingly, musical theater scholars have begun to note the predisposition of musicals toward embodied reception, what Stacy Wolf terms a particularly "performative spectatorship" (Wolf, 2002, 33). Audiences for musicals do not simply watch and listen; they engage kinesthetically, from the most subtle head movement, to tapping fingers to the beat, to feet mimicking dance steps under a chair. And as D. A. Miller points out, this embodiment isn't limited to the actual moments of watching. Many audience members who might hum under their breath during the show offer their own performance of a number later on.[8] Of course, as musicals move into the home via television and DVD, official performances and audience performances can merge. If you are watching alone in your living room, singing full voice and dancing along with a number won't disturb anyone!

The 2008 Pixar film *Wall-E* offers an entertaining illustration of this concept. Wall-E, a trash-compacting robot left alone on earth after all humans have fled, has acquired and become attached to a recording of the musical film *Hello, Dolly*. As the film opens, we see that Wall-E sometimes collects and saves interesting objects during his compacting rounds, including, on this day, a round disc. When he returns home and plays the recording, we see why he chose this object: he wanted to be able to perform along with a sequence of the musical that involved hats. It's clear, watching this moment, that Wall-E has made a regular practice of performing along with the recording and that he has forged a deep connection to the movie that goes far beyond simple entertainment. Watching a musical isn't enough, even for a futuristic robot—the embodiment of reception is somehow essential.

Live, participatory screenings of film and television musicals, most notably *The Rocky Horror Picture Show* (1975), present a different type of embodied reception. This film adaptation of the stage musical *The Rocky Horror Show* was initially unsuccessful before it began to be presented at midnight showings in 1976. These screenings quickly became popular live performance events in their own right, with audience members participating by responding, vocally and physically, to the movie, as well as performing along with the film in floor shows, often in costume.[9] Like Wall-E, audiences for *Rocky Horror* seem compelled to perform along with the musical, but here those performances are social, interactive, and vocal, as well as physical. As both these examples indicate, musical theater scholars need to think more about what it means to take musicals into our bodies. How does this mode of reception affect the ways in which audiences make meaning from musicals? What are musical audiences embodying, as they tap their toes and sing along?

And who are the audiences for musicals? On one level, the answer is almost everyone in the United States—and beyond. Because musicals are a commercial, popular form, they are widely produced in community theaters, dinner theaters, and high schools, and are also a common mode of performance for churches and community festivals. When people ask about the audience for musical theater, however, they are most often referring to Broadway musicals. At the Museum of the City of New York, a placard in the ongoing exhibit *Perform: A History of Broadway and Theater in New York City* describes Broadway's audience as "relatively well-off, well-educated, and predominantly white and female. Visitors to New York fill the largest percentage of seats." Statistically, this assessment is probably true, at least in the early twenty-first century. According to a report by Broadway's national trade association, from June 2006 to June 2007 Broadway audiences were 64% female and 74% white; they had an annual household income averaging just under $100,000, and of those over twenty-five, 75% were college graduates. Tourists accounted for 65% of ticket sales.[10]

We should, however, think carefully about how this sort of quantitative data may (or may not) be useful. We might believe, for example, that we can draw significant conclusions about musicals and gender based on these demographics. We know from the statistics that more women than men attended Broadway musicals in 2006–07. We also know that in the popular imagination, the form is typically positioned as somehow associated more with femininity than masculinity, regardless of content, and it would be easy to assume that the audience numbers have created this perception of the form. It would be equally easy, however, to use these data to support an argument that musicals are *designed* to appeal to women and their assumed femininity, and are succeeding. The fact that both of these presumptions come easily to mind points out that the numbers themselves tell us only that a relationship exists; they can tell us almost nothing about how that relationship works, or where causation lies.

Also lacking from the picture created by the demographic study is any recognition of the relationship of gay men to musical theater, which also influences perceptions of effeminacy. The perceived feminization of musical theater accrues not only (or even, I would argue, primarily) from the majority-female audience but also from the affiliation of musical theater with gay men. David Savran echoes many other scholars when he notes that "musical theater . . . has in popular mythology been adjudged a sacred preserve of gay men."[11] More specifically, musicals are commonly affiliated with effeminate gay men, as in the stereotype of the "show queen." D. A. Miller, like John Clum and other scholars, emphasizes the interrelationship of musicals, gay men, and a queered experience of gender. Miller argues that musical theater functions as "a form whose unpublicizable work is to indulge men in the thrills of a femininity *become their own*" (Miller, 90). While Miller sees a femininity inherent in musicals that makes them appealing to gay male audience members, I would suggest that a more complicated, cyclical relationship is at play: musicals respond to audience interest *and* to perceptions of that interest, and audiences respond both to actual qualities of musicals *and* to perceptions about musicals. While statistics can tell us something about the sex (and sexuality, were that question added) of audience members, they can't unpack this cycle. Quantitative data, therefore, is of limited value in understanding the relationship of musical theater and gender to audiences.

The numbers we have regarding "the Broadway audience" also don't really address the distinct audience makeup for any particular show. The 2008 audience demographics for *Passing Strange* (2008), for example, a coming-of-age story about a young black musician featuring a rock score by its star, Stew, likely differed from those for *Phantom of the Opera* (1988), Andrew Lloyd Webber's operatic megamusical based on the novel by Gaston Leroux. When one is writing about a particular show, awareness of those demographics could potentially be useful. For example, research on *Passing Strange* might benefit from attention to the demographic makeup of the audience and how it differed—or not—from the larger Broadway audience, in order to investigate the show's particular appeal. However, the causation problem would remain. While we can make educated guesses, it's important to resist oversimplifying the relationship between show and demographic. For example, *Phantom of the Opera* has been running for decades, at this point offers very little in the way of theatrical innovation, and has had an enormously successful national and international marketing campaign, while *Passing Strange* had a short run that followed a successful Off Broadway engagement, considerably less aggressive marketing, and more experimental elements in its dramaturgy. All of these things play a role in who fills the theater seats, alongside any emphasis on identity markers like race or age within the show itself.

This points to what is perhaps the largest weakness of using statistics to study audiences. Statistics address questions relevant to marketing a musical, but they can tell us very little about how audiences find meaning in musicals. In the end, what does knowing that 68% of the audience for a given show is female tell us about how spectators engaged with the production? Identities are complex and intersectional; the category of "woman," for example, includes such an extraordinarily diverse range of identities and experiences that it becomes almost meaningless as a way of understanding viewing practices. Simply put, sharing a single identity category doesn't mean that spectators will have the same or even similar responses. As Stacy Wolf notes, engaging with a performance requires us to draw on our "cultural competencies," which "are developed in everyday life and can include identity positions . . . *as well as other kinds of knowledge*" (Wolf, 2002, 25, emphasis mine). While demographic identity markers influence some of our cultural competencies, others derive from experiences and knowledge bases outside traditional understandings of identity. For example, when I watch musicals, my knowledge of musical theater history and interest in directing typically influence my interpretation and response more than any of the traditional identity categories into which I fit.

It's also important to recognize that we can take up viewing positions that may not match our identity category. Perhaps the best example of this is the practice of "queering." In queering, spectators read, watch, or listen in queer ways to a text that officially contains no queer content. For example, an audience member watching *Chicago*'s Velma attempt to seduce Roxie into forming a double act might read her efforts as seduction of a more literal type. Alexander Doty asserts that queer readings are not limited to people who identify as gay, lesbian, bisexual, or queer, and he argues that queer readings and responses can occur "whenever *anyone* produces or responds to culture" (Doty, 3). In making her case for lesbian and feminist readings of mid-century musicals, Wolf makes a similar point, noting that these readings are not limited to lesbians and women (in fact, she acknowledges that some lesbians and women will have no interest in such readings at all) but are available to anyone with sufficient cultural competency and interest (Wolf, 2002, 5). In the end, queering offers an excellent example of the limits of identity's value in understanding reception practices.

None of this, of course, is meant to ignore the very real role identity politics can play in bringing audiences to the theater. We are often drawn to entertainment that features characters that we understand as somehow "like us," whether that means African American audiences attending *The Color Purple* (2005) or younger audiences flocking to *Rent* (1996). A production's marketing choices can also influence these trends. For example, *Rent* pioneered the practice of offering heavily discounted ($20) tickets for the first two rows of orchestra seats to whoever would wait in line for them.[12] This innovation encouraged younger audience members, who couldn't necessarily afford ordinarily high ticket prices but often had both the time and inclination to accept long, sometimes overnight, waits, to attend. It's also worth noting that a show's audience makeup may shift over time, as hits such as *Phantom of the Opera* or *Rent* accrue cultural capital and become "the thing to see," whether or not the show itself seems particularly interesting to a given spectator.

CRITICS

Critics, adversarial or supportive, have been essential collaborators throughout musical theater's history. Throughout the Golden Age of musical theater, New York had up to nine daily papers publishing theater reviews, including the *New York Times*, the *Herald Tribune*, the *Daily News*, the *Post*, and the *World-Telegram and Sun*. Critics' feedback could encourage changes in a show during its tryout period, influence a show's journey to Broadway, increase (or decrease) attendance, and help shape audience response. During out-of-town tryouts, reviews from local critics had two crucial effects. First, they offered the creative team outside perspectives on what was— or wasn't—working. Since revisions were an expected part of these tryouts, critics could have significant influence on how a show evolved. Second, they helped create expectations and word of mouth for the show as it moved toward Broadway.

For much of musical theater's history, critics' reviews were vital to a show's success once it arrived in New York. Unanimous bad reviews were typically enough to close a show, while strong reviews were seen as essential to creating a hit. Carol Channing, reminiscing about her first starring role, in *Gentlemen Prefer Blondes*, emphasizes the degree to which a show's success or failure was seen as dependent on the critics: "After the show, I could not leave my dressing room until . . . all the powers that be had advance notice from the newspapers that we were a hit."[13] The prestige of the reviewer, and particularly the paper he wrote for, mattered; if reviews were mixed, the *New York Times* often proved a decisive voice. The power of the *Times* has only increased in recent years, as the number of daily papers in New York has continued to drop. Still, as important as reviews have always been, they aren't perfect predictors of a show's box-office potential. Well-reviewed shows don't always have long runs—the original production of *Candide* (1956), for example, received mainly positive reviews but closed after a money-losing seventy-three performances.[14] While, as this suggests, reviews have never been 100% predictive of success or failure, the power of traditional print criticism has also waned over time. Some contemporary shows leave critics unimpressed but wow audiences and become smash hits. (I'll talk more about one example, *Wicked* [2003], at the end of the chapter.) Conversely, *Passing Strange* was a critical success, with strong reviews including a rave from Charles Isherwood in the *Times*, but it ran only 165 performances.[15] There is one area, however, in which critical power seems to have increased over time. While negative reviews no longer lead to automatic closure, today's critics can help a show open. Increasingly, musicals are developed off Broadway, often by nonprofit theaters. Strong reviews of these shows frequently encourage producers to invest in a Broadway production.[16]

While traditional criticism clearly retains some influence, in recent years the major print critics have ceased to be the only game in town. New media platforms have created increasing opportunities for criticism that can both add to the historical archive and influence an ever-wider body of potential audience members. In particular, the rise of the Internet has provided new forums for criticism. First, as most newspapers add online platforms to their print work, the "official" review becomes accessible to those who may not subscribe to the paper. Many papers' Web sites also allow readers to comment and post their own thoughts. The *New York Times*, for example, puts links to their critic's review and user reviews side-by-side on the page of show listings. Anyone who is interested can easily move from reading Isherwood's review of the hit musical *Spring Awakening* (2006) to perusing the ninety-two "user reviews" posted by interested audience members.[17] A more personalized criticism is available via e-mail. While people have always been able to obtain reviews from friends, the advent of e-mail makes the process quicker, simpler, and more easily archived. A request for reviews can be sent out once to a wide variety of friends and colleagues, who can respond immediately. Their responses, more easily than phone conversations, can then be saved for future use.

The advent of other online media have also increased opportunities for less official, but often no less astute, criticism. Blogs, for example, allow for more specialized criticism that explicitly takes up particular points of view. The immensely popular social networking site Facebook also offers opportunities for recreational criticism. While a Facebook account includes a profile with basic biographical information, users can also download applications to personalize their pages, including "Stage Door," which allows users to display their favorite shows and review them. Finally, a less textual but as easily archived online venue for criticism is the podcast. Podcasts are audio (and increasingly, video) recordings that interested listeners can download free of charge. Fairly easy to create, podcasts offer another avenue through which recreational critics can reach out to anyone with an interest in musical theater. Like blogs, podcasts tend to be ongoing affairs, allowing listeners to become familiar with the critic's point of view. It's important to remember, too, that these platforms can offer access to productions done in any venue a writer cares to address— from Broadway to small town high schools—thereby offering students of musical theater access to information on small, local productions that ordinarily might be difficult to study.

While the particulars of critics' power and the media through which they communicate have shifted over time, critics remain crucial to our understanding of musical theater history, as reviews provide what is often the only record of what a production might have looked and sounded like. However, we have to remember that those records are neither objective nor transparent windows onto the performance. In examining a given piece of criticism, it's crucial to consider the writer's goals. Different critics have different understandings of the critic's role. Some recognize that they are creating a historical record and emphasize details in order to archive what otherwise will exist only in memories. Many see themselves as a commercial service, helping audience members decide how to spend their money. Some consider themselves guardians of an art form and focus on enforcing what they see as its standards, "polic[ing] the boundaries of the cultural hierarchy" (Savran, 2003, 48). Still others are interested in using theater, and musical theater specifically, to hold conversations about larger world issues. Of course, these aren't mutually exclusive objectives, and most critics combine two or more of them. Given the limited word count available for their responses, critics' choices of goals have enormous influence on what they include in their writing.

Considering a critic's objectives is the first step in using his or her work productively. The second is paying attention to a particular critic's interests and strengths. For example, Walter Kerr, critic for the *Herald Tribune* from 1951 to 1966 and later for the *New York Times*, was a book writer for musicals before he was a critic, making his dramaturgical assessments particularly interesting. Awareness of a critic's tastes and biases is also helpful. Some critics mark these themselves. Clive Barnes's (*New York Times*) 1977 review of *Annie* offers an amusing example. He notes his surprise at finding the show "whimsically charming," since he typically has no patience for shows about "performing children and performing dogs." His positive review, he points out, should therefore be read differently from one by a writer who "customarily swoons at" such material.[18] In other cases, it may be necessary to do a little research. Does a critic typically adore a particular performer? Dislike deviation from the traditional book musical form? Find a given composer uninspiring? Reviewers' opinions on any specific show are best understood in the context of their larger bodies of work.

Finally, it's useful to look at as many reviews of a production as possible. Different reviewers may take entirely different views of a given show, or they may disagree on specific elements. Reviews of the 1980 revival of *Camelot*, for example, range from raves to absolute pans. Critics also split widely on Richard Burton's star performance. While Frank Rich, in the *Times*, rhapsodized about how Burton "seems to own [the stage] by divine right" and found his reprise of his 1960 performance magnificent, Clive Barnes in the *Post* was positively nasty: "he seems little more than a burnt-out dummy." Clearly we can't draw any conclusions about the overall quality of Burton's performance through these reviews. Several reviewers, however, mention the unique and powerful quality of Burton's "sonorous" (Barnes), "powerful yet vulnerable" (Rich), "distinctive, irresistible voice" (Watt, *Daily News*).[19] So while we can't judge his performance as a whole, we can safely assume that Burton's vocal performance was strong and distinctive, and we can begin to imagine what it might have sounded like. Through careful, thoughtful use of reviews, musical theater scholars can begin to recreate performances lost to time without inadvertently codifying a single individual's opinions or biases.

AUDIENCE–CRITIC INTERSECTIONS: *WICKED*

I conclude by looking briefly at a recent musical as an example of the complicated interactions among musicals, audiences, and critics. *Wicked*, the blockbuster success that opened in 2003, offers a useful perspective on these relationships, in part because of how the production constructs its audience. All theatrical performances, including musicals, address themselves to a particular type of spectator, with particular cultural competencies. This choice of address is not naïve or innocent; as I noted at the beginning of the chapter, as a commercial form, musicals are produced, particularly on Broadway, to bring in audiences large enough to fill houses and earn a profit. Still, shows are increasingly choosing to target spectators outside the traditional "white, middle-class, heterosexual, and male" (and, I would add, middle-aged) paradigm mainstream theater has typically emphasized.[20] Looking at *Wicked*'s engagement with its intended audience outside as well as inside the theater, alongside its relationship to critics, will clarify some of my earlier arguments and offer an example of how we might begin to think about musical theater audiences and critics in more nuanced ways.

An adaptation of Gregory Maguire's novel of the same name, *Wicked* reimagines the story of *The Wizard of Oz*'s Wicked Witch of the West. The musical focuses on Elphaba, the green-skinned girl who will become that feared figure—unjustly, in this version—and follows the development of her friendship with Galinda/Glinda, the Good Witch. While Glinda and Elphaba have heterosexual romances, it is their relationship that forms the spine of the show. *Wicked*, then, unapologetically focuses not just on women, but on young women. As Wolf notes, it taps into "a contemporary lexicon of 'girl power' images."[21] Additionally, by emphasizing Elphaba's role as an outsider, the show speaks to challenges most young people face as they move into adulthood. Attention to the show's merchandising strategies bears out an interest in attracting young, female fans: the "Ozdust Boutique" homepage, the hub for online sales of *Wicked* merchandise, primarily features young women in fitted T-shirts.[22] While T-shirts for male fans can be found deeper in the Web site, much of the merchandise is distinctly feminine—pink T-shirts, sparkly earrings and necklaces—and the models, particularly the women, generally seem much younger than the "average" Broadway audience member. *Wicked* aims squarely for a young, female audience.[23]

Indisputably a hit, *Wicked* continues playing as of this writing to nearly 100% capacity crowds in New York almost eight years after opening, with productions finding significant success in other cities and on tour.[24] Yet it opened to reviews that were mixed, at best. Brantley, in the *Times,* found things to admire—particularly Kristin Chenoweth's performance as Glinda—but in the end his review, tellingly titled "There's Trouble in Emerald City," described *Wicked* as a "bloated production" that "does not, alas, speak hopefully for the future of the Broadway musical."[25] Isherwood, writing for *Variety*, had similar feelings.[26] The *New Yorker*'s John Lahr was also impressed by Chenoweth and a few other elements, but he found the score lacking and saw *Wicked* as "a morass of overproduction." He concluded his review by mocking audience members who "gave this fourteen-million-dollar piece of folderol a standing ovation."[27] In the *Village Voice*, Michael Feingold's scathing review labeled the show "a hideous mess of a musical."[28]

One critic, however, gave the show a glowing review. Elysa Gardner, theater and pop music critic for *USA Today*, declared *Wicked* a "triumph" and "the most complete, and completely satisfying, new musical I've come across in a long time."[29] There are likely many reasons for Gardner's divergence from her colleagues: her taste in music, her relative interest (or lack thereof) in upholding cultural hierarchies, or any number of other factors. Still, it's perhaps telling that she is the lone female critic represented here. Watching the 2007 documentary *Show Business: The Road to Broadway*, which follows four new musicals and a set of critics through the making of the 2003–04 Broadway season, it's impossible not to notice that almost all the critics chosen to represent their field are middle-aged (or older) white men.[30] It's equally impossible not to notice a certain tone of disdain (echoed in some of the reviews cited) for *Wicked* and its fans, a disdain that seemed absent when they questioned or doubted other shows. It seems plausible that at least some of this hostility may have come from being in the unusual position of finding themselves emphatically *not* the ideal, targeted spectator for this particular musical.

In considering why *Wicked* was able not only to survive these negative reviews but also to thrive like few other musicals in history, the difference in cultural competencies between the audience the show spoke to most directly and the official critics seems particularly relevant. Perhaps audiences were so willing to ignore the official reviews because they also recognized that *Wicked* wasn't aimed at those critics. Certainly, other factors helped make the show a success despite the sometimes nasty reviews. It's an adaptation of a very popular novel, itself an adaptation of a classic American film, based on a classic popular novel. It offers enormous spectacle, something that has often proven quite appealing to audiences. And the Internet allowed for the creation of an enormous fan community, building enthusiasm and extremely positive word of mouth from audience members who, knowingly or not, were taking on the role of critic themselves—and doing so from an ideal, rather than a marginalized, spectatorial position.[31] The convergence of all of these factors makes *Wicked* a useful example of the need for nuanced, multifaceted analysis in considering the interconnected relationship between audiences, critics (professional and recreational), and musicals.

NOTES

1. http://education.yahoo.com/reference/dictionary/, accessed July 11, 2009.
2. See David Savran, "Toward a Historiography of the Popular" (*Theatre Survey* 45 [2004]: 211–17).
3. Susan Bennett, *Theatre Audiences: A Theory of Production and Reception*, 2nd ed. (London: Routledge, 1997), p. 21.
4. For more on the relationship of audiences to these popular culture media over time, see Richard Butsch, *The Making of American Audiences: From Stage to Television, 1750–1990* (Cambridge: Cambridge University Press, 2000).
5. In fact, beginning with *Jesus Christ Superstar* (1971), some musicals released cast albums prior to the production itself, creating fans before the show was ever performed.

6. Stacy Wolf, *A Problem Like Maria: Gender and Sexuality in the American Musical* (Ann Arbor: University of Michigan Press, 2002), p. 7. See also Michael R. Schiavi, "Opening Ancestral Windows: Post-Stonewall Men and Musical Theatre" (*New England Theatre Journal* 13 [2002]: 77–98).

7. Joss Whedon, "Liner Notes," *Buffy the Vampire Slayer: Once More, with Feeling, Original Cast Album* (Rounder Records, 2002), p. 3, emphasis mine.

8. D. A. Miller, *Place for Us: Essay on the Broadway Musical* (Cambridge, MA: Harvard University Press, 1998), p. 87.

9. See Raymond Knapp, *The American Musical and the Performance of Personal Identity* (Princeton, NJ: Princeton University Press, 2006), pp. 240–52. Among several book-length accounts of the *Rocky Horror* "phenomenon," see especially Jim Whittaker's *Cosmic Light: The Birth of a Cult Classic* (Altoona, PA: Acme Books, 1998).

10. *The Demographics of the Broadway Audience 2006–2007*, Broadway League, http://www.broadwayleague.com/index. php?url_identifier=the-demographics-of-the-broadway-audience-2005–2006, accessed September 13, 2008.

11. David Savran, *A Queer Sort of Materialism: Recontextualizing American Theatre* (Ann Arbor: University of Michigan Press, 2003), p. 59. See also Miller; Wolf, 2002; John Clum, *Something for the Boys: Musical Theater and Gay Culture* (New York: St. Martin's Press, 1999); Alexander Doty, *Making Things Perfectly Queer: Interpreting Mass Culture* (Minneapolis: University of Minnesota Press, 1993); Frances Negrón-Muntaner, "Feeling Pretty: West Side Story and Puerto Rican Identity Discourses" (*Social Text* 63 18.2 [2000]: 83–106); and Schiavi.

12. Matthew Blank, "Broadway Rush and Standing Room Only Policies," *Playbill. com*, http://www.playbill.com/celebritybuzz/article/82428.html, accessed December 2, 2008.

13. Carol Channing, "Foreword," in *Opening Nights on Broadway: A Critical Quotebook of the Golden Age of the Musical Theatre, Oklahoma! to Fiddler on the Roof*, by Steven Suskin (New York: Schirmer Books, 1990), p. xv.

14. Steven Suskin, *Opening Nights on Broadway: A Critical Quotebook of the Golden Age of the Musical Theatre, Oklahoma! to Fiddler on the Roof* (New York: Schirmer Books, 1990), p. 132.

15. Charles Isherwood, "It's a Hard Rock Life: Theatre Review of *Passing Strange*" (*New York Times* [February 29, 2008]). http://theater.nytimes.com/2008/02/29/theater/reviews/29stra. html?ref=theater. (accessed May 9, 2011).

16. I wish to thank Steven Adler for his assistance with this point.

17. "Broadway," http://theater2.nytimes.com/venues/broadway.html, accessed November 24, 2008.

18. Clive Barnes, "Stage: 'Annie' Finds a Home" (*The New York Times* [April 22, 1977]: 65).

19. As quoted in Steven Suskin, *More Opening Nights on Broadway: A Critical Quotebook of the Musical Theatre, 1965 through 1981* (New York: Schirmer Books, 1997), pp. 131–33. Both this volume and its precursor, *Opening Nights on Broadway*, offer useful overviews of the critical response to a vast array of Broadway musicals (although the reviews are heavily edited), as well as brief biographies of major critics.

20. Jill Dolan, *The Feminist Spectator as Critic* (Ann Arbor: University of Michigan Press, 1988), p. 1.

21. Stacy Wolf, "'Defying Gravity': Queer Conventions in the Musical *Wicked*" (*Theatre Journal* 60.1 [2007]: 1–21), pp. 4–5. Wolf also argues compellingly that the relationship the show builds between the two young women is a queer one.

22. "The Ozdust Boutique Online," *Araca Merchandise*, http://www. wickedmerch.com, accessed September 13, 2008.

23. *Wicked* was not the first show to address a young, female audience, but its success has inspired more shows with a similar approach. See Campbell Robertson, "Tweens Love Broadway, but Can't Save It Alone" (*New York Times*, October 2, 2007). http://www.nytimes.com/2007/10/02/theater/02twee.html?pagewanted=1&sq=tweens%20love%20broadway&st=nyt&adxnnl=1&scp=1&adxnnlx=1304978860-IUYelSXsiF3Nk8z0abvYWQ. (accessed May 9, 2011).

24. "Broadway Grosses: Wicked," *BroadwayWorld.com*, http://www. broadwayworld.com/grossesshow.cfm?show=Wicked, accessed May 7, 2011.

25. Ben Brantley, "There's Trouble in Emerald City: WICKED" (*New York Times* [October 31, 2003]: E-1).

26. Charles Isherwood, "More Bothered than Bewitched by *Wicked*" (*Variety* [November 3, 2003]: 30).

27. John Lahr, "The Critics: The Theatre: Bitches and Witches: Ulterior Motives in *Cat on a Hot Tin Roof* and *Wicked*" (*New Yorker* 79.34 [November 10, 2003]: 126–27).

28. Michael Feingold, "Voice Choices: Theater: Green Witch, Mean Time: Both On and Off-Broadway, New Musicals Suffer from Severe Multiple Personality Disorder" (*Village Voice* 48.45 [November 5–11, 2003]: 77).

29. Elysa Gardner, "Something 'Wicked' Comes to Broadway" (*USA Today* [October 31, 2003]: 9E-6).

30. *Show Business: The Road to Broadway*, directed by Dori Berinstein, 2007 (Liberation Entertainment DVD release, 2007).

31. For an excellent discussion of *Wicked*'s relationship to its girl fans, see Stacy Wolf, "Wicked Divas, Musical Theatre, and Internet Girl Fans" (*Camera Obscura* 22.2 [2007]: 39–71).

7

Stars and Fans

HOLLEY REPLOGLE-WONG

■ □ ■

Sawyer, you're going out a youngster, but you've got to come back a star!

—42nd street (1933)

AMERICAN IMAGINATIONS HAVE INVENTED NUMEROUS mythologies about the fledgling Broadway star ascending to her or his rightful place in the show business firmament. *42nd Street,* Busby Berkeley's Depression-era "backstage" film musical, tells the quintessential "big break" tale. A young chorus girl, Peggy Sawyer (Ruby Keeler), gets an opportunity of a lifetime when she is selected to replace the lead, who broke her ankle the night before the premiere. With a singular stroke of luck, and a lot of hard work to develop her raw ability, the chorus girl becomes a star on the Great White Way overnight—and every member of the onscreen audience is thrilled that they were the lucky ones who were able to witness, and participate in, the birth of the star. The film ends with the audience leaving the theater abuzz with adulation for the new leading lady.

Although Sawyer's exhilarating rise to fame is a fictional tale, it has several points of articulation with a real and equally thrilling legend. Midway through the evening of October 14, 1930, a young unknown singer and former secretary who had purportedly "never had a singing lesson in her life" took center stage at the end of the first act of George and Ira Gershwin's *Girl Crazy* and introduced her second featured solo of the evening, "I Got Rhythm."[1] The fast-paced, rhythmically exhilarating tune played up Ethel Merman's best asset as a performer: her powerful belt voice that she could project, loud and clear, straight into the back of the theater. On the second time through the chorus, Merman omitted the first three lines of lyrics and triumphantly belted a sustained C over the orchestra before demanding "Who could ask for anything more?" Indeed, the audience decided that they couldn't, and Ethel Merman was an overnight sensation. Audiences responded to her ability and powerful presentation. Critics broadened audiences' acclaim with notices that drew in even more people wanting to be dazzled by the new talent. In short time, Merman's name would headline Broadway theater marquees.

Both of these star-making mythologies assimilate and reconcile seemingly paradoxical aspects of stardom. Sawyer and Merman are both "ordinary people"—an average city-dweller and a stenographer—with extraordinary raw talent. They work hard (in *42nd Street*, Sawyer works to near collapse; the consummate professional Merman sings her songs the same way every time and was famous for rarely requiring an understudy) but also win success because of a lucky "break"— one critical opportunity to show the world what they can do. Although stars have modest and relatable roots, they must also be exceptional enough to receive notice. Stars are accessible, but also extraordinary. Merman's "natural" vocal ability and alleged humble background (really a middle-class upbringing) provides hope to dreamers. And although they may have "what it takes" to be a star, they need the audience to accept them, identify with them, and idolize them in order to thrive.

Richard Dyer, who pioneered the field of star studies in his influential book *Stars*,[2] outlines some of the incongruities that form a star's persona. As Stacy Wolf points out, "The star persona is a public figure who is defined, often complexly and often with contradictions, in relation to the cultural politics and social practices of her time."[3] A star may reify the ideological status quo by reiterating or concealing dominant values, but he or she can also be a locus for resistance or subversion, a place of identification for the marginalized audience member (Dyer 1998, 26).[4] Star-making is a reciprocal project that is mediated between the star figure (including the entourage of agents, managers, and stylists), the media, the mass audience, and the individual fan. These elements work together to create the star's image, which is the persona that the public sees and consumes. Stories about stars enact a capitalistic American narrative of success. As Dyer writes, "The general image of stardom can be seen as a version of the American Dream, organized around the themes of consumption, success, and ordinariness" (Dyer 1998, 38). Star legends provide inspiration and optimism, but stardom does have its dark side as well. Dyer cites Judy Garland and Marilyn Monroe as two examples of the "soured" American dream, stars whose enduring mythologies are as much shaded by personal and professional tragedy as they are highlighted by success.

Success in the two star scenarios related here (one fictional, one not) relies as much on adoration from the audience as it does on the talent of the performer. A star's image is made up of media "texts," including not only roles and performances but also artifacts such as recordings, films, publicity pictures, and interviews. Fan practice and the relationship between fans and star texts are intricate and varied. In this essay, I outline an introduction to scholarship on stars and fan participation in stardom, and I address a variety of topics pertinent to the study of stars and fans of musical theater. What characteristics compose a star? How do stars operate socially and culturally? How does a star leave an imprint on a show text? How do audiences participate in fandom? I also consider the history of stardom in musical theater, detailing how facets of stardom and the relationships between stars and fans have been altered as recording technologies changed.

STAR QUALITIES

So, what is a musical theater star? Perhaps it may seem silly to ask this question because much of what defines a star is obvious and easy to identify; audiences "know" who has achieved stardom. Although the "star," the "celebrity," and the "diva" often seem to be interchangeable terms, since they all suggest fame and power, these classifications have important differences. Celebrity suggests renown and notoriety but does not imply the talent, ability, and continued existence as a figure of importance that a star might have. A diva has an extraordinary aura of talent, endurance, and a strongly defined persona. More generically, a star is a public figure (often a performer) whose personal fame is foregrounded as much as or more than the roles he or she plays. Stars are multivalent personae; they are people who work as actors who portray characters. Stars combine distinctive talents with recognizable (and often imitable) looks and personalities that are spun and perpetuated as an image. A star's image is not limited to visual content; the voice, manner of speech, and patterns of behavior are all part of celebrity. It is not enough to be perfect for the role, or a gifted "triple-threat" (singer, dancer, and actor). Stars are unique. Their voices and personae are recognizable, and their abilities and charm are not only impressive but often somehow off-kilter: Ethel Merman's brashness and big belting voice, Julie Andrews's primness and carefully balanced vocals, Patti LuPone's quirky diction, George Hearn's hammy acting and booming lyric baritone.[5]

Visibility is certainly a factor of celebrity; a star typically has a resumé filled with leading roles in successful and popular shows (although perhaps a few flops as well; one of the most important facets of a diva persona is her ability to triumph over failure with a spectacular comeback). Stars are marketable; their names come above the show title on the marquee, as an incentive for audiences to buy tickets. Successful stars like Bernadette Peters or Audra MacDonald sell tickets to solo concert performances with their names alone. Without star power, these performers might have successful careers, but they would not be the major draw; the show would take precedence.

Richard Dyer writes, regarding film stars, that image develops from media texts such as interviews, publicity photos, and recordings, which

> consist both of what we normally refer to as his or her "image," made up of screen roles and obviously stage-managed public appearances, and also of images of the manufacture of that "image" and of the real person who is the site or occasion of it. [6]

In Dyer's view, stars are always significations; the public never knows them as "real people," although the fact that stars are also people who have offstage lives raises questions of authenticity and authorship that the fan must process and reconcile. Celebrity media work hard to convince the public that what we are seeing is private and "real life." Behind-the-scene biographies and interviews practice acts of "authentic spontaneity." To what degree do stars author their images, and to what degree are the roles they play reflective of their selfhood? Audiences want to know who the person is, and they often believe that the star's image is representative of his or her actual self. Stars perform roles based on a "good fit" to their personae (playing types), and we map readings of the actor onto the character; but the oeuvre of accumulated roles also offers possible readings of the star.

Musical theater is full of female stars with strong, diva-like personae, and the repertory of shows favors strong women performers. But what is a "diva?" The term "diva," borrowed from both an Italian word ("goddess") and the Latin *divus* ("divine one"), was initially applied to late nineteenth- and early twentieth-century operatic sopranos. Historically, "divas" are women performers; the term is rarely applied to male performers except in reference to a gender-bending or queer performance (as with a drag queen, for instance). Not all female musical theater stars are divas, and it is possible for a diva's star to fizzle. In order to reach "divadom," a diva must have been a star at some point in her career, but she can still retain the diva label even if her star is no longer in ascendance.

The voices of past and current divas are inextricably bound up in notions of genius and embodiment. Divas are not only figures of fascination but potentially also figures of public identification through their public personal struggles and tragedies. In addition to diseases and addictions, career battles and personal strife, often publicized with reference to her appearance and weight, the diva must show resilience and the ability to make a comeback against steep odds. Judy Garland, with comebacks both tragic (her 1954 film *A Star is Born*) and triumphant (her 1961 Carnegie Hall concert) codified these tragic qualities of the diva for twentieth-century popular music audiences.[7] Beyond their highly iconic images and mannerisms, singer-divas have historically thrived on talent, extravagance, and unique, innovative vocal styles. The diva also displays an apparent indifference to reality, which may be a result of her total unawareness of how she is being received or a misunderstanding of what audiences find appealing about her.[8] However, this indifference often comes across to the public as courage and grit, and in the end the diva sometimes turns to a sort of rueful acknowledgment of her reception in her public persona.

A BRIEF HISTORY OF STARDOM

Historically, the emergence of stardom is often traced to eighteenth-century theatrical actors, particularly David Garrick, whose star mythology reads similarly to the ones above: his innovative naturalistic portrayal of Richard III in 1741 brought him fame nearly overnight. In the 1790s, actors following in the footsteps of Garrick toured popular roles (often Shakespeare) through Europe and the United States, promoting themselves just as much as, if not more than, the roles they played. They fused their names to the character so audiences could easily remember and spread the word about an individual actor's version of the character.[9]

Through the early nineteenth century in the United States, actors were typically employed as stock players attached to a particular theater. Actors specialized in certain types of role, and they would rotate between playing leads and character parts, depending on the cast list and genre of the play; an actor who played the romantic lead in one play with the company might have nothing to do with the next play, featuring a comic male lead. As more stars became known and toured more frequently (often European actors like Sarah Bernhardt), stock companies went into decline. Stars were a stronger audience draw, and they helped "legitimize" the theatrical profession to a public who had long been suspicious of actors' morality. Actors who were acclaimed for their interpretations of dramatic roles provided an image of greater stability than the nameless stock player, and through them the public slowly began to regard theater as a respectable profession and stable economic venture.[10]

In 1817, European vocal stars began to tour American theaters, singing selections from famous operas in variety shows and solo concerts. One of the most popular vocal stars was the "Swedish Nightingale," soprano Jenny Lind, who had a wildly successful American concert tour in 1850, engineered by circus impresario P. T. Barnum. She was famed as much for her charity, Victorian-era virtue, and "anti-diva" behavior as she was for her voice, which was celebrated for being pure and clear, possessed of very little vibrato or excessive emotion. Her voice was a reflection of her carefully constructed public persona; as Susan Leonardi and Rebecca Pope point out, Lind "provided middle-class ticket buyers with a model of their own ideals."[11] She performed only in venues appropriate to her image of respectability, such as concert halls and churches. Her image was part of the product audiences consumed, and it was both relatable and exceptional.

Through the nineteenth century, concert tours like Lind's and touring companies with hopeful performers crossed America. Variety and minstrel shows were itinerant, of irregular quality, and attracted varying audience demographics; some were held in community theaters, others in saloons. Minstrel shows in particular were geared toward a mostly white, male, working-class audience. In 1860, theaters across America started to organize a tour schedule for variety shows, and performers developed their acts to target family audiences, creating the genre of entertainment known as vaudeville. By the 1890s, vaudeville performers traveled to a set series of theaters—a "circuit"—and depending on their style and quality, they would be hired to perform in "small time" venues (low-paying contracts, frequent performances, rural theaters) "medium time" theaters, or the "big time" urban theaters that catered to the middle and upper classes. Theaters decided the lineup of the acts based on quality and popularity; the best acts went on second (when the audience was finally seated) and second to last, and the worst acts went on first (while people would be looking for their seats) and last (to clear out the theater). This system inherently leaned toward the development of a star system: acts that were familiar, well advertised, and reviewed were the ones that generated more revenue and word-of-mouth promotion.

Sheet music of popular songs, which were generally sold to middle-class amateur musicians, was marketed with a picture of the star who had made the tune famous on the cover. Performers rose and fell on the circuit—the more popular the act, the better lineups and bookings it received. The genre of American musical theater came into its own at the end of the nineteenth century, developing from both European operetta and forms of music theater such as minstrelsy, vaudeville, burlesque, and the spectacular extravaganza (the 1866 extravaganza *The Black Crook* in particular figures into the beginning of American musical theater).[12] Stars from vaudeville were often the first headliners in these productions. George M. Cohan, for instance, a "writer-director-star" who grew up touring vaudeville circuits with his family, was one of the early developers of Broadway shows in the 1900s.

Cinema took its first audiences and many of its first actors from vaudeville and the so-called "legitimate" stage ("artistic" theater, as opposed to "commercial" theater) where the star system was already in place. Janet Staiger points out that in early film studios, actors were not given name credit (they were labeled by a production company: for example, "The Vitagraph Girl"), but eventually studios were pressed by the public to adopt the cult of personality as the main source of publicity for their output. Audiences had a stronger curiosity about the stars—what their lives were like, where they shopped, whom they spent time with—than the production companies had anticipated. To audiences, stars had become a significant part of what defined entertainment.

With the advent of the "talkie" (films with synchronized sound), screen adaptations of musicals gave audiences across America the chance to enjoy professionally produced musicals with stars they might not otherwise have been able to see if their city was not big enough to warrant a national tour and if they lacked the funds and leisure time to visit Broadway. The first big success of sound film, *The Jazz Singer* (1927), starring Al Jolson (perhaps the biggest vaudeville star of all time), established this pattern. That film and many that followed gave even small-town audiences the opportunity to experience a star's "presence." Later breakthroughs in commercial recording technology each placed a different set of demands on the star and changes in the ways in which fans might engage with them. A significant swath of scholarship on stardom focuses on film, which has become the benchmark of stardom in American culture, the site where true stars test their box-office mettle. Musical theater has a number of important points of historical articulation with film studies—perhaps inevitably so, given the early run of successful filmed musicals.

STARS AND TECHNOLOGY

The Jazz Singer established the musical as a commercially viable genre for the screen, and it also set a precedent for the musical to become a star-focused form of entertainment. Studios developed "stables" of musical stars, and studio musicals were crafted to showcase the talents of their most popular stars, who served as a kind of name-brand guarantee of a certain kind of product; audiences trusted stars to give them a quality product in their specialized genres. Fred Astaire had achieved stardom on Broadway when he signed with RKO, and the studio teamed him with Ginger Rogers as supporting players in *Flying Down to Rio* (1933). Their dance number in that film made them stars of the silver screen, and RKO went on to produce nine musicals for them within the span of six years (1933–1939). At MGM, Judy Garland, who started her career as part of a touring sister act in vaudeville, struggled against her studio-manufactured image of the unglamorous, extremely talented, eternal little girl. Gene Kelly, an established dancer and choreographer on Broadway, came to Hollywood in 1941 and became an innovator for cinematic dance in films such as *An American in Paris* (1951) and *Singin' in the Rain* (1952). Some musical theater stars did not transition well to the screen; Ethel Merman and Mary Martin each made a few films and left Hollywood, never achieving the kind of success they enjoyed on Broadway.[13] However, while Merman's and Martin's performance styles and personae did not translate well to the screen, they came across well as guest performers on live television.[14] Early television variety shows borrowed conventions of form and style from vaudeville and had live studio audiences; musical theater actors were accustomed to playing to an auditorium of spectators.

In the 1950s and '60s, starring roles in a handful of important film musicals went to Hollywood stars whose singing voices, inadequate by normal Broadway standards, were either overdubbed or left alone as an emblem of naturalness; the former included Natalie Wood in *West Side Story* (1961), Rosalind Russell in *Gypsy* (1962), and Audrey Hepburn in *My Fair Lady* (1964), and the latter Marlon Brando in *Guys and Dolls* (1955) and Lee Marvin and Clint Eastwood in *Paint Your Wagon* (1969). Ironically, Julie Andrews won an Academy Award for *Mary Poppins* (1964) in the same year she had been denied the lead role in the film adaptation of *My Fair Lady*, which she had originated on Broadway. Barbra Streisand became a film star with her 1968 screen debut as Fanny Brice in a film adaptation of *Funny Girl*, a role she created on Broadway, but she had already found popular success as a singer, stage actress, and recording artist. Liza Minnelli, another star who was involved in several kinds of media at once—live performance, recordings, film, and television—reached a pinnacle of fame in 1972 when she starred in a film adaptation of *Cabaret*.

More recent film musicals continue to cast current screen stars as their leads, some of whom lack the singing and dancing chops to do well on Broadway but still acquit themselves well on screen (e.g., Nicole Kidman in *Moulin Rouge!* [2001] and Johnny Depp in *Sweeney Todd: The Demon Barber of Fleet Street* [2007]; Catherine Zeta Jones in *Chicago* [2002], trained as a dancer but known primarily as a film star, was on the other hand a "surprise" talent). Other film musicals borrow celebrities from popular music, like Jennifer Hudson and Beyoncé Knowles for *Dreamgirls* (2006). This practice parallels a current trend on Broadway, where starring roles in running shows and revivals are occasionally filled by Hollywood stars (such as Brooke Shields in *Cabaret*), pop idols (Usher and Ashlee Simpson in *Chicago*), and reality show favorites (Clay Aiken in *Spamalot*). Familiarity with Broadway stars no longer has the same level of mass culture currency as it did during the Golden Age of musicals; it has become a kind of specialized knowledge, and both film and musical theater producers look to mass media celebrities to energize their box office earnings.

Radio broadcasts reached mass audiences, and record sales brought stars' voices into people's homes, where the nuances of their voices could be consumed and enjoyed repeatedly. In 1943, Decca Records released a six-disc original-cast album of *Oklahoma!*, the first recording of a musical with the entire original cast and orchestra. The record was packaged with plenty of pictures of the stars and the stage production, and an insert describing the plot. The success of the *Oklahoma!* album spurred the production of cast albums for other shows, and cast albums have since become important artifacts to fans, who can imagine and recreate a star's performance in their homes, whether they were able to see the production or not. Recordings offer fans a sense of intimacy and familiarity with a star; listening at home can be both intimate (listening closely, perhaps with headphones) and interactive (singing and dancing along).[15]

Following the introduction of amplified sound in musical theater—first crudely with corded microphones in the first runs of *Hair* (1967) and *Jesus Christ Superstar* (1971), and more complexly with the headset microphones and mixing technology of the megamusical in the 1980s—stars no longer needed to have voices that projected into the back of a large auditorium, and audiences grew impatient with non-amplified sound. Although amplified performers' voices are disconnected from their bodies and physical locations—voice are picked up, mixed, and sent out into the theater through speakers—audiences have become more accustomed to amplified, mixed sound as emblematic of reality (as in film) and seem to prefer it to the realism of a voice directly produced from an actual body on the stage.[16]

STAR VEHICLES

The 1959 musical *Gypsy* was tailored from its inception as a vehicle for Ethel Merman, a show that would be written both to suit her talents and to stretch her dramatic chops (to convince critics to rethink their long-held complaints about her weak acting). The show was based on the memoirs of burlesque strip artist Gypsy Rose Lee, but the drama of the show focuses on Gypsy's mother, a stage mother to end all, Madame Rose. Ethel Merman had a significant role in the early planning stage of the show and used her power as a star to influence the selection of the creative team. Merman and producer David Merrick discussed the possibility of turning Lee's memoir into a show, and after Merrick obtained the rights to Lee's book, he approached Jerome Robbins to direct and Leland Hayward (at

Merman's request) to co-produce. Arthur Laurents was eventually persuaded to write the book, and Robbins asked Stephen Sondheim to write the score. Merman, however, did not want a then-unknown composer writing the music and brought in Jule Styne, confining Sondheim to the role of lyricist once again.[17]

As noted above, character narratives merge with star images, so that Rose was understood by audiences as an articulation of something essential about Merman's private self: "Merman's powerful sound is the perfect expression of Rose's character: loud, forceful, unyielding."[18] John Clum calls *Gypsy* a diva musical: a show that glorifies its female star, is authored in part by important gay artists (Stephen Sondheim and Arthur Laurents) and provides a locus of identification for the gay male spectator (especially the closeted audience of the 1960s). The narratives of this kind of show tend to eschew love stories in favor of tales about women's independence and survival—the specialties of the diva. Since its first run, *Gypsy* has had four Broadway revivals. Finding the right actress to play a role that was tailored to a star with very specific abilities is a complicated feat—how does a casting director find another Ethel Merman? The solution for all four revivals was to cast another diva possessing a similar larger-than-life persona, but with a different voice and acting style to bring to the role. *Gypsy* has since become a vehicle for other stars, an opportunity for them to reinvent Madame Rose. Only a woman of a certain age and status can do Rose, and it is a challenge to her divahood. To the fan, the character in the drama matters less than the opportunity to see how the star will take on the role.[19]

When *Gypsy* was adapted as a film musical in 1962, film actress Rosalind Russell was cast in the lead role, and her singing was dubbed. Merman was crushed when she did not get to play Rose on screen, but she took *Gypsy* on national tour while the film was in production. The first star to tackle the role on

Broadway after Merman was Angela Lansbury in 1974. She was already an established actress in Hollywood, and a Broadway star since her career-defining turn in the title role of another diva-musical, *Mame* (1966). She had won a Tony Award for her star turn in the otherwise critically panned musical *Dear World* (1969). Her famed contribution to the performance practice of *Gypsy*, in collaboration with Jerome Robbins, was to "solve" the applause problem at the end of Madame Rose's climactic breakdown in "Rose's Turn." Although the music ends triumphantly, Rose is still desperately broken, and the writers felt that applause would be inappropriate for the drama. They had convinced Merman to continue with the scene and forfeit her applause, but Oscar Hammerstein II persuaded them to let the applause happen—at least to give the audience the chance to cathartically express their appreciation. When Robbins and Lansbury worked together on a London production, they allowed the applause to happen, but Lansbury's Rose remains lost in her fantasy and continues to bow after the applause has ceased, reminding the audience that they are watching a woman in the midst of an emotional crisis.[20] That Lansbury was the star who figured this out suggests that she is a different kind of star from Merman, resisting diva impulses for the sake of the drama. This anecdote reifies a broadly accepted "fact" about Merman's personality: that she is always concerned with being center stage, regardless of who or what she has to maneuver into the background.

In 1989, television actress Tyne Daly took on the role, and she self-consciously reimagined Madame Rose's stage mother as a woman who has spent half a lifetime convincing herself that she didn't make it as a stage performer because she was "born too soon and started too late"—although it becomes clear in her delivery of the monologue before "Rose's Turn" that she never made it because she simply wasn't good enough.[21] Bernadette Peters's 2003 Rose had the archetypical toughness but was also attractive and vulnerable.[22] Patti LuPone's performance, like Merman's, was tagged as monstrous (in Charles Isherwood's estimation, LuPone's interpretation was monstrously sexual).[23] In an important way, the performance is really no longer about the role itself, that is, the character in the drama, but rather about the audience's desire to watch a star taking on the role and making it her own, and seeing that reflexive give and take between the diva and the diva role.

FANDOM AND FAN PRACTICE

The two star stories at the beginning of this essay have an unsung key player: the audience. As I indicated above, audiences have a stake in a star's image, and the perspective of the fan is an important position to engage with when thinking about a star. Fans are much more than "spectators"—passive consumers of media texts.[24] Audiences and individual fans are interactive components in the creation and reading of stars; they are part of the image-making process, and although they may not have direct input in the signals stars send out, they can choose what they wish to engage with. A fan has a personal engagement with a star's image, and his or her perspective will be shaped by experience and personal demographics. Dyer argues that the allure of the star is in the ways that the star image is constantly in dialogue with the tensions between public and private spheres—the star embodies (or idealizes) certain social identities, and a star's performance of "social categories" helps individuals understand themselves within society.[25] Fans may also choose to share their experiences by participating in an interactive community developed from a shared attachment to a star. Fan community may be broadly defined; it may be a small group of friends with a shared passion, or an Internet message board with active members from around the world.[26]

Musical theater is a genre that is popular with both mainstream and marginalized audiences. It has historically had a significant gay male following; D. A Miller, in *Place for Us*, writes that nearly all the 1950s musicals—a genre that appears assuredly hetero-normative on the surface—have subtext that validates gay audiences.[27] Recently, teenage girl fans—an audience that has a history of being dismissed by mainstream critics—have emerged as a more visible audience for the musical with the blockbuster success of Stephen Schwartz's *Wicked*.[28] These diverse fan communities have varied and endless ways of interpreting musical theater star texts and engaging with their fandom. For instance, a fan may keep track of a star's career and personal life; he or she might study, imitate, and emulate a star's performance style or dissect the particulars of a performance (whether a recording, a stage production, an appearance in a film, or a live televised event) with fellow fans.

Scholarship on fans and fandom is a relatively recent development in academia, and one that produces considerable strain between the supposedly polarized "moral values" of the scholar and the fan. If a scholar is supposed to be "objective," how can she comprehend and fairly portray what it means to be a fan, and likewise, can a scholar trust fans to articulate what is important about their participation in fandom? It is important to note that the meaning of fandom changes among different social and cultural groups. As Matt Hills writes:

> I want to suggest that fandom is not simply a "thing" that can be picked over analytically. It is also always performative; by which I mean that it is an identity which is (dis-)claimed, and which performs cultural work. Claiming the status of a "fan" may, in certain contexts, provide a cultural space for types of knowledge and attachment.[29]

In academia, labeling oneself a fan carries the risk of having one's work disparaged for lack of critical engagement. However, as Alexander Doty argues, it may also be problematic for scholars to suppress their personal alignments for the sake of an imagined academic professionalism.[30] One solution taken by scholars has been to embrace their "scholar-fan" subjectivity and acknowledge their positioning as they theorize fandom, as in the work of John Clum, Henry Jenkins, or Matt Hills. Fan ethnographies are another method used by scholars such as Jackie Stacey and Janice Radway, who foreground the individuality of fans and allow their voices to shape their scholarship.[31]

Internet fan sites and discussion boards are important locations of community for fans, making ethnographic research over the Internet a useful way of engaging with fans from different geographic locations in dialogue within online communities. Community and school theater programs are also likely to have knowledgeable and passionate fans who aspire to emulate their favorite stars. Recordings of musical theater stars inspire ambitious young singers to imitate their sound and style—a complex consequence of technology. Original cast performers codify how the show is supposed to sound, and amateur performers typically choose to model their own styles on what they have experienced from the cast album. Imitating the voice allows the fan to own something essential of the performer that would otherwise be impossible to experience. Stars in turn summon aspiration and ambition from their followers. Would-be stars emulate the star's vocal style, delivery, and physical mannerisms while they imagine the glamour of the star's life and fantasize about their lives if they had the star's talent, beauty, wealth, and power. Fans desire to hear the voice, but in some way, they also want to *own* the voice.[32] Ownership may be earned in a number of different ways: repeated listening, publicly performing the diva's music in school or community shows, or in more private spaces, by lipsynching or dancing at home.[33]

Some shows develop fan cults that track favorite performers across national tours and replacement casts. In the cast of *Wicked,* young fans track their favorite actresses who have played Glinda and Elphaba and savor brief moments of difference from the "canonical" cast album, for these moments seem to unlock some small part of the performer's personality. Consider, for instance, the penultimate measure in the act I finale, "Defying Gravity." The commercially available sheet music and the original cast album have different versions of Elphaba's melisma, but it is Idina Menzel's melisma, which she likely devised to showcase her high belt to thrilling effect, that persists as "canon." However, different touring actresses devise their own melismas: a stamp of their individuality.

Part of the power of stars is the illusion that the fan can be intimately familiar with their lives; the fan with a certain level of vocal ability can own her voice, perform her music, relate to her, and share in her success. Following in the footsteps of Fox's "American Idol" and the recent placement of former Idol contestants in Broadway shows, the pop culture phenomenon of reality television has "gone Broadway" with shows like "Grease: You're the One That I Want" (2006) and "Legally Blonde the Musical: The Search for Elle Woods" (2008). Susan Smith, discussing the BBC contest show "How Do You Solve a Problem Like Maria?" (2006), posits the reality show as a possible solution to the problem of casting leads for a show such as *The Sound of Music,* which has an iconic star performance perhaps too difficult for the audience to overcome or "forget."[34] Although choosing the contestant most similar in image to Julie Andrews, the audience gets a seemingly real experience of "direct participation" in star-making; they get to know the contestant and watch the Sawyer- or Merman-like process from nobody to star, and in the case of the *Grease* and *The Sound of Music* shows, even vote for their favorite to win. The process of identification is thereby reified and intensified. After all, the reality show contestant could conceivably be any one of us; any one of us could become a star.

NOTES

1. A common feature of Merman's star mythology is that she had never received formal vocal training, and further, that George Gershwin advised her never to do so after her success in Girl Crazy. Caryl Flinn, Brass Diva: *The Life and Legends of Ethel Merman* (Berkeley: University of California Press, 2007), pp. 31–32.
2. Richard Dyer, *Stars* (London: British Film Institute, 1998).
3. Stacy Wolf, *A Problem Like Maria: Gender and Sexuality in the American Musical* (Ann Arbor: University of Michigan Press, 2002), p. 34.
4. Richard Dyer, *Stars* (London: British Film Institute, 1998), p. 26.
5. Within Andrews's persona, vocals always serve the role; see Peter Kemp, "How Do You Solve a 'Problem' Like Maria von Poppins," in *Musicals: Hollywood and Beyond*, ed. Bill Marshall and Robynn Stilwell (Portland: Intellect, 2000, pp. 55–61), and Stacy Wolf, *A Problem Like Maria: Gender and Sexuality in the American Musical* (Ann Arbor: University of Michigan Press, 2002).
6. Richard Dyer, *Heavenly Bodies* (London: Routledge, 2004), p. 7.
7. *A Star Is Born* (1954) was brutally edited for its theatrical release, in part because the studio worried about its running time and the attention span of the average audience member. The film did not make its expected profits. Garland was also denied the Oscar that year, even though the Academy went through the trouble of setting up a live feed into her hospital room so she could be "present" at the event. Her concert in Carnegie Hall on April 23, 1961, was one of the highlights of her career, and the recording won five Grammy awards.
8. Mae West, for example, is beloved for her audacity and her drag queen mannerisms, but nonetheless she insisted on her (decidedly nonmainstream) sexiness until the end of her career.

9. See Dyer, 1998, 91, and Jean Benedetti, *David Garrick and the Birth of Modern Theatre* (London: Methuen, 2001).

10. See also Janet Staiger, "Seeing Stars," in *Stardom: Industry of Desire*, ed. Christine Gledhill (London: Routledge, 1991), pp. 3–16, and Katherine K. Preston, "American Musical Theater before the Twentieth Century," in *Cambridge Companion to the Musical*, ed. William A. Everett and Paul R. Laird (Cambridge: Cambridge University Press, 2002), pp. 3–28.

11. Susan J. Leonardi and Rebecca A. Pope, *The Diva's Mouth: Body, Voice, Prima Donna Politics* (New Brunswick, NJ: Rutgers University Press, 1996), pp. 44–45.

12. Regarding *The Black Crook* and its historical importance to American musical theater, see Raymond Knapp, *The American Musical and the Formation of National Identity* (Princeton, NJ: Princeton University Press, 2005), pp. 20–29.

13. See Stacy Wolf, *A Problem Like Maria: Gender and Sexuality in the American Musical* (Ann Arbor: University of Michigan Press, 2002), for a consideration of why these women had trouble assimilating as Hollywood stars.

14. The two appeared on many television variety shows and in June 1953 sang a duet medley of their greatest hits for the Ford fiftieth anniversary special, remembered as a momentous event in musical theater star history.

15. The voice of the singer is a commodity indebted to the listener. Leonardi and Pope discuss the potential for a recording of a diva's voice to become a fetish object when separated from the body as a recording and "circulated in a masculine economy" (Leonardi and Pope, 195).

16. Regarding the "cinematizing" and changing aesthetics of sound in the megamusical, see Jonathan Burston, "Theatre Space as Virtual Place: Audio Technology, the Reconfigured Singing Body, and the Megamusical" (*Popular Music* 17.2 [1998]: 205–18).

17. See Meryle Secrest, *Stephen Sondheim: A Life* (New York: Alfred A Knopf, 1998).

18. John M. Clum, *Something for the Boys: Musical Theater and Gay Culture* (New York: Palgrave, 1999), p. 169.

19. See John Clum's analysis of the 1998 Gypsy revival at the suburban Paper Mill Playhouse in New York, with Betty Buckley playing Rose.

20. Arthur Laurents, *Original Story By: A Memoir of Broadway and Hollywood* (New York: Alfred A. Knopf, 2000), pp. 395–96.

21. Both Lansbury and Daly won Tony Awards for their turns as Madame Rose. Merman was nominated but lost to Mary Martin (Maria in *The Sound of Music*). There are two filmed versions of *Gypsy*, the 1962 adaptation starring Rosalind Russell and the 1993 version with Bette Midler.

22. Arthur Laurents, liner notes to *Gypsy* (original revival cast album CD, Angel Records 7243-5-83858-2-3, 2003).

23. Charles Isherwood, "Patti LuPone in Gypsy: Light the Lights, Boys! Mama Rose Hears a Symphony" (*New York Times* [August 15, 2006], http://theater.nytimes.com/2006/08/15/theater/reviews/15lupo.html, accessed April 9, 2011).

24. Jackie Stacey argues that film theories of spectatorship ignore the spectator's social context to study the ways that film texts produce "spectator positions," while cultural studies investigate "audiences' readings" of texts. Film theory regarding stars has historically given agency to the "text" (i.e., the film) rather than the audience, privileging the term "spectator," which carries a connotation of audience passivity. Jackie Stacey, *Star Gazing: Hollywood Cinema and Female Spectatorship* (London: Routledge, 1994).

25. He also raises the possibility of reading stars as camp, since they exaggerate conventional "types," as in the hyper-sexuality of Marilyn Monroe.

26. For related arguments on fan culture, see Henry Jenkins, *Textual Poachers: Television Fans and Participatory Culture* (London: Routledge, 1992), p. 49.

27. D. A. Miller, *Place for Us* (Cambridge, MA: Harvard University Press, 2000). See also Clum.

28. See Barbara Ehrenreich, Elizabeth Hess, and Gloria Jacobs, "Beatlemania: Girls Just Want to Have Fun Beatles," in *The Adoring Audience: Fan Culture and Popular Media*, ed. Lisa A. Lewis (London: Routledge, 1992), pp. 84–106, and Stacy Wolf, "Wicked Divas, Musical Theater, and Internet Girl Fans" (*Camera Obscura* 65 22.2 [2007]: 39–71).

29. Matt Hills, *Fan Cultures* (London: Routledge, 2002), pp. xi–xii.

30. Alexander Doty, *Flaming Classics: Queering the Film Canon* (London: Routledge, 2000), p. 11.

31. Besides other work cited here, see Janice Radway, *Reading the Romance: Women, Patriarchy and Popular Culture* (Chapel Hill: University of North Carolina Press, 1984).

32. Wayne Koestenbaum argues that the diva's identity lies in her voice, a product of her effort that is also a component of her body. Wayne Koestenbaum, *The Queen's Throat: Opera, Homosexuality, and the Mystery of Desire* (New York: Poseidon Press, 1993).

33. See Miller. For closeted Golden Age Era boys, this practice is encoded as gay; see, for instance, Matt Damon's private lip-synching performance in *The Talented Mr. Ripley* (1999, dir. Anthony Minghella), and the reaction of Dickie Greenleaf (played by Jude Law).

34. Susan Smith, unpublished contribution to "You Gotta Have a Gimmick": Startexts and Voices" (panel presentation at "The American Musical on Stage and Screen: An Interdisciplinary Extravaganza," University of California, Los Angeles, October 2007).

8

Knowing your Audience

JENNIFER CHAPMAN

■ □ ■

THIS ESSAY INVESTIGATES THE SHARED history and contemporary practices of community and high school musical theater in the United States, through which each has established a unique relationship to its audience—an audience that has in turn shaped its identity and informed its musical selections. Critical scholarship about amateur theater suggests its viability as a form of civic engagement,[1] as a subversive space where the "masses" own the means of production,[2] and as the primary disseminator of theater knowledge and experiences in the United States.[3] Documentation of practices in community and high school theater suggests that each offers an experience that is very different from, but equal in value to, professional theater.[4]

DOCUMENTING PRACTICE

Unfortunately, there are few case studies, personal narratives, or documentary studies of community and high school theater practices.[5] However, there is an abundant source that offers a kind of "back door" into the subject: "how-to" resource manuals written for teachers, directors, and producers of amateur theater.[6] Although they vary in quality and level of critical engagement, many of them are written by practitioners and so offer valuable anecdotal evidence about what "works" in amateur theater, how audience expectations shape ideological boundaries of community and high school musical theater production, and what practicalities amateur theater makers face in selecting, casting, and producing plays.

Between 2001 and 2004, the American Association of Community Theatres (AACT), with its umbrella organization, Theatre USA, collected documented histories of community theaters in the United States, including play and musical production since 1919. The resulting publication, *Millennium Theatres: Discovering Community Theatre's Future by Exploring Its Past*, includes theater members' personal memories, records of ticket sales, stories or descriptions of how theaters were restructured to meet economic or community needs throughout the years, and useful anecdotal evidence of the challenges and rewards of participating in community theater.[7]

Another resource for documenting practice is *Dramatics* magazine. Published by the International Thespian Society (ITS) and the Educational Theatre Association (EdTA), *Dramatics* targets high school students and their teachers, and compiles from member schools a "most produced play and musical" list annually. While *Dramatics* does not provide an exhaustive look at all high school theater work in the United States, it represents schools that have made a commitment to including theater in their curricula or after-school activities.

An inventory of the play lists in *Millennium Theatres* and *Dramatics* shows that the top shared musical titles for community and high school production are *Guys and Dolls* and *Oklahoma!* The remainder of this essay investigates why Broadway musicals are so popular in each venue and how these two shows offer possibilities and challenges when they function, in part, as a way of building community and facilitating civic engagement.

REACTING TO AND EMBRACING BROADWAY

The intersecting histories of community and high school theaters in the United States arguably bind them to similar ideological assumptions and expectations about their processes and products. Both forms developed alongside the "little theater" movement in the early twentieth century and were also influenced by the development and expansion of theater programs in universities. Both became popular, in part, because of a growing belief that theater's creative process has educational and social value.[8]

From about 1912–1920, theater companies known as "little theaters" were created throughout major cities in the United States, using professional directors and amateur actors and staff, who sought to provide an alternative to popular commercial (Broadway) productions and to experiment with European forms, especially the "free theater" movement. The little theater movement was an important nurturer of playwrights such as Eugene O'Neill and Susan Glaspell; it is regarded as a key contributor to the development of a uniquely American dramatic voice. It planted the seed from which other amateur theater forms grew, such as community, high school, and university theater.[9] These forms owed much of their public support to the little theater movement, which introduced the idea that amateur theater can have a powerful impact on its participants and broader grassroots community. Yet, although the little theater movement sought to offer an alternative to Broadway, community and high school theater has generally chosen to produce known Broadway titles.

Another reason for the growing popularity of theater at the local level, particularly in high schools, was the expansion of theater programs and classes at the university level. As more newly certified teachers graduated from universities after taking courses in theater, they disseminated that training into secondary classrooms and local communities.[10] According to Kenneth Macgowan, writing for *Harper's* in 1929, "drama is the new thing in the high schools," estimating that "probably a third of the twenty-two thousand high schools in America are studying and applying production methods to a rather decent grade of play." Macgowan commends the youth of 1928 for their work in theater, declaring that, based on his observations of high schools, "Broadway theatre may be dying, but never was the theatre so alive in the rest of the United States" (Macgowan, 1929, 774, 779). While it unclear how Macgowan arrived at his numerical estimate, his article highlights the role that theater and drama, particularly Broadway musicals, came to play in transforming the American high school and its local communities.

ONE HISTORY BECOMES TWO: ORGANIZATION AND EXPANSION

Louise Burleigh introduced the term "community theater" in 1917, describing it in *The Community Theatre in Theory and Practice* as "a house of play in which events offer to every member of a body politic active participation in a common interest" (Burleigh, xxiii). By 1925, a community theater movement was thriving, with 2,000 companies registered with the Drama League of America, a professional organization formed in 1910 to support the development of community theater.

Theater work in American high schools appeared as early as the mid-1920s. The 1920s were a time of debate and change for secondary school curricula, primarily because of problems in recruiting and holding students. Early advocates of high school theater production and study argued that it benefited students' moral, social, and academic development (Hume and Foster, 1932; Law, 1936; Macgowan, 1921; W. Brown, 1947). The introduction of theater into the secondary curriculum was part of an effort to attract and retain a larger student body and to teach life skills that would make students "better" Americans in various ways (Chapman, 2005; Chapman, 2007; Hume and Foster, 1932).

By 1928, the national curriculum was revised to meet the needs of "all" students rather than just an elite, college-bound group. The new curriculum placed the social on a par with the scientific, and subjects were offered that taught "effective living." Twelve fields of instruction were available: English, foreign language, math, science, social studies, business, manual/industrial arts, agriculture, home economics, (visual) art, music, and physical education.[11] An emphasis on students' moral development as good Americans and their responsibilities to the welfare of society's future provided a rationale for theater to enter secondary school. Educators argued that by performing good citizenship and ethical decision-making in dramatic enactments, students could rehearse the roles of their future, adult selves.[12] Initially, theater was studied as part of "oral interpretation" in English classes, but in some schools this small subset of an academic course was expanded into play production, playwriting, and even schoolwide competitions (Macgowan, 1921, 174–75). The National Thespian Society, a nonprofit organization dedicated to the advancement of secondary school theater, was formed in 1928, gained a membership of seventy schools within its first year, and by 1939 tallied 33,000 student members.[13]

The period following World War II was one of the most economically expansive in American history, to the great financial benefit of community arts and arts education. The expansion of community and high school theater work during this period is evident in the establishment and growth of professional organizations to represent both forms and a growing critical interest in the role of amateur theater in local communities.

The American Community Theatre Association (ACTA) was created in 1956 to represent community theaters at the national level; at that time, there were an estimated 3,500 community theaters across the United States (Gard and Burley, 1959), a number that would grow to 15,000 by 1975.[14] Renamed the American Association of Community Theatres (AACT) in 1986, the group currently represents 7,000 member companies in the United States and in the armed forces overseas. It publishes resources, offers support to members in their organizational needs, sponsors an annual competitive festival of community theater performance, and sends select member companies to competitive theater festivals internationally (http://www.aact.org).

Since Burleigh's initial definition of "community theater," a number of amateur theater movements—such as "little," "tributary," "fringe," "community-based," and "alternative" theater—have blurred the boundaries of what constitutes "community" theater. The term today is used broadly to describe amateur theaters supported by local communities on stage, backstage, and in the audience. Currently, the AACT defines a community theater as a nonprofit, tax-exempt organization staffed (onstage, backstage, and in its administrative structure) primarily by volunteers (http://www.aact.org). However, this definition is merely a guidepost, since different communities provide different levels of financial support for local theater. Some community theaters have funds to pay one or more individuals, such as a full- or part-time managing director, or an occasional set designer, stage or musical director, or conductor. Rarely does payment represent a full-time livable salary, and it seems uncommon to pay performers. As nonprofit, tax-exempt organizations, community theaters may support themselves with local, state, or national grants; they may rely on community donations; and they likely depend heavily on ticket sales, particularly to subscribers.

During and shortly after World War II, the National Thespian Society saw a significant increase in school memberships and active participation. Between 1941 and 1950, schools reporting to the annual play survey increased from 729 to 1,548. With increased participation came more critical articles in *High School Thespian* (the official publication of the National Thespian Society, renamed *Dramatics* in 1944) about how and why theater should be practiced in school settings. Articles from the mid-1940s through early 1960s tend to focus on pedagogy and play selection, offering assistance to teachers looking to create or improve theater programs and giving students a sense of national solidarity. The latter concern is evident in the January 1951 "Dedication," which also documents an explosion in the number of schools participating in the play survey:

> This issue of Dramatics—our ninth Pictorial number—is dedicated to the largest play cast in the world—the twenty thousand high school boys and girls, who, as Thespians, practice our motto: "Act well your part: there all the honor lies." By being loyal / To their fellow classmates / To their directors and teachers to their school / To their parents / To their community / To their country. [15]

Moreover, in 1945 and 1949, the "High School Committee" of the American Education Theatre Association (which would later become EdTA) published pedagogical guidelines for secondary theater study: "Teaching Dramatic Arts in the Secondary Schools" (1945) and "Course of Study Materials for a High School Dramatics Course" (1949). The latter was published in the *National Association of Secondary School Principals' Bulletin* and disseminated to its membership at their annual conference.[16]

Today, the National Thespian Society is called the International Thespian Society (to recognize a small Canadian membership), and its publication for members, *Dramatics* (titled *The High School Thespian* until 1944), is distributed to about 42,000 individuals, 80% of whom are high school students. The remaining 20% comprises theater teachers, librarians, and other interested individuals.[17] The International Thespian Society is currently under the umbrella of the Educational Theatre Association (EdTA), which publishes and distributes *Dramatics* and, along with the American Alliance for Theatre and Education (AATE), represents teachers of high school theater, guided by state and national theater arts standards that define "highly qualified" theater teaching under the No Child Left Behind Act.[18]

A COMMON CHALLENGE: NEGOTIATING EXPECTATIONS

As noted, community and high school theater differs from the little theater movement in tending to produce known Broadway titles, particularly musicals. Although community and high school theater programs face unique challenges in play selection, they share some important commonalities—particularly in their audience makeup—that lead to similar choices for production. In both, many audience members are likely to know (or have some personal connection to) a person who worked on the show and would not attend otherwise. Since many audience members are also likely to know one another, attendance may be thought of as a form of civic engagement. Audience makeup is likely broad; parents, grandparents, siblings, and children are all important supporters of friends and family members who worked on the show. Finally, since some audience members are potential future participants, productions serve partly as a kind of "audition" to the community they serve.

Guidelines in "how-to" texts for community and/or high school theater indicate that both spaces must consider similar audience expectations. Texts suggest that to be successful, programs should (1) offer shows that audiences of all ages can attend, (2) omit or criticize onstage behavior that may be viewed as inappropriate or immoral by the community at large (such as smoking, drinking, doing drugs, using vulgar language or violence, etc.), (3) sanitize images of sexuality and avoid references to homosexuality (except perhaps for the purpose of a joke, since making fun of homosexuals has often been sanctioned implicitly by schools that do not address homophobia and heterosexism with students), and (4) try to create entertaining and fun community-building events (Chapman, 2005, 2007). Community theater audiences seem to tolerate slightly racier material than high schools. (For example, *The Fantasticks*, a documented popular choice for community theater, includes a song about a rape, but several texts about how to produce high school theater suggest cutting this number.) Nevertheless, guidelines tend to reinforce heteronormative behavior in male and female characters and present courtships with predictably stereotyped gender behavior.

Historically, both community and high school theater have been identified as spaces of civic engagement and opportunities to teach or profess what it means to be a "good American."[19] Specifically, in 1921, observing the educational possibilities of high school theater, Kenneth Macgowan stated that "acting is being used deliberately by the teachers as a means to correct defects in the personalities of the students and to build a better citizenship" (774). And in 1932, Hume and Foster argued that the process of creating theater has educational value and the potential to uphold democratic principles when it is created for and by students (30–39).

Selecting material for community and high school theater has always been a careful negotiation between the needs of participants and audience members. Historically, community theater has had to compete with other forms of live entertainment, such as sporting events, fairs and carnivals, and traveling tent shows. High school theater has often been challenged by competing opinions about what is "appropriate" for that age group. In the past and present, familiar works from the commercial stage have helped guarantee an audience and excite potential participants.

Selecting material for community theater is often difficult. Sometimes it is done by a board of directors, sometimes by the directors and/or membership, and sometimes a combination of the two. The selection process can lead to conflicts over the mission and identity of the theater and the community it serves. Audiences have strong expectations that their community theater will produce Broadway musicals, at least occasionally, and reward them with high ticket sales when they do (Filichia, 2007).

Broadway musicals are also a staple of many high school theater programs in the United States. Parents, administrators, and student bodies expect a musical production to integrate music, dance, and drama departments (or clubs), with the drama teacher usually given the job of directing it. Ample evidence for this expectation may be found in the number of "how-to" teacher resource texts for directing high school musical theater and the recent inclusion of an "acting in musical theater" section in *Dramatics* magazine.

One of the unique problems of teaching and directing theater with high school students, both historically and in contemporary practice, lies in the question of what is "appropriate" material for the age group. This is a challenge faced by theater and drama teachers of all youth-age groups because often teachers, administrators, parents, and students hold different opinions. For example, in 1947, Wilhelmina P. Brown wrote in *Dramatics*:

> The fact remains that in a public school we of the teaching staff must cater, or at least defer, to the religious and moral sense of our parents and patrons. We must not permit any of the student actors to smoke on the school stage. We must not show the effects of, or indicate the drinking of alcohol. We must not use profanity. These are the unwritten requirements that a high school production must abide by. . . . Rarely will you find a parent who is proud to see his offspring caricature a drunk. [20]

Although audiences' tolerance of content may have shifted since 1947, the problem remains one of balance: is it possible to provide teens with quality artistic experiences while appeasing society's desire to preserve their childhood innocence? Broadway musicals, particularly those from the "Golden Age" of American musical theater, offer a safe choice, in addition tending toward large ensemble casts and offering opportunities for collaboration with dance and music departments. [21]

In contemporary practice, high school theater production tends to be guided by the following ideological assumptions: (1) theater has the potential to teach "life skills" and is thus important beyond its ability to teach within its discipline; (2) productions will be something that students, parents, and younger siblings can attend; (3) student actors should not engage in onstage behavior that is not allowed in the school at large (such as smoking, drinking, doing drugs, using vulgar language or violence, etc.); (4) plays should not be overtly sexual or have nonheterosexual characters (unless for the purpose of a joke); and (5) theater class or drama club is an alternative to playing sports and thus occupies an "unmasculine" space in high school society (Chapman, 2005, 2007).

Community theater is often affected, if not guided by, similar expectations. However, Leah Hager Cohen (2002) shows, in *The Stuff of Dreams*, how challenging these expectations can lead to productive dialogue. She tells the story of a conflict within the Arlington Friends of the Drama (AFD, a seventy-five-year-old community theater in Arlington, Massachusetts) over the desire of its younger members to produce David Henry Hwang's *M. Butterfly*. Older members object to the play's use of onstage nudity and its central characters' same-sex relationship. The younger contingency, led by a director with a vision to take the play to state and national competitions, wins the debate and the play is produced. Amazingly, members of the faction against producing the play do not abandon their volunteer work and continue to make coffee, clean the theater, and promote the show despite wholeheartedly being against it (189–217, 218–234). Cohen shows how a community theater's play selection process can be a site for public debate about the community's values and can serve as the vehicle through which a community can understand and articulate its changing identity (5–9). The same can be true for high school theater; when teachers negotiate with their principal, school board, and community to produce risky shows (such as *Rent*), they educate other adults about the issues that contemporary teenagers confront in real life.[22]

A SHARED CANON

The overwhelming popularity of certain shows, as documented by the AACT, Theatre USA, and the Educational Theatre

Association, has created a de facto canon for musicals in community and high school theater; this canon in turn reveals some expectations that audiences have of each form. Broadway musicals from the Golden Age tend to dominate this canon, but note that focusing on the "most popular" musicals documented by these organizations does not consider either individual theaters' full seasons, which might also include riskier work, or nonmember school and community theaters. Looking at a documented canon provides merely one means for assessing popular trends in these venues.

In *Millennium Theatres*, AACT-member companies report the work of Gilbert and Sullivan (specifically, *H.M.S. Pinafore, The Pirates of Penzance, Princess Ida,* and *The Mikado*) as the most popular choices from 1919 to 1950 (*Millennium Theatres* does not distinguish between Gilbert and Sullivan societies and other community theaters). After 1950, the majority of reported musical productions are from Broadway. The ten most popular plays for community theater, as documented by Theatre USA and AACT, in order of popularity, are *The Fantasticks; Guys and Dolls; Oklahoma!; Fiddler on the Roof; The Sound of Music; The Wizard of Oz; South Pacific; The Music Man; A Funny Thing Happened on the Way to the Forum;* and *Godspell.* Many of these most popular titles are from the Golden Age and are categorized in Peter Filichia's *Let's Put on a Musical* as "good old reliable" shows:

> As Coca-Cola discovered some years ago, people like classics. So if you too are in a community that buys tickets only for the most famous titles in the Broadway canon, here are your bread-and-butter musicals. (Filichia, 2007, 7)

Clearly, most of the AACT-member theaters indeed have to make some bread and butter with their musical productions. Catering to such needs, Filichia groups musicals according to considerations more practical than historical. For example, he discusses *The Sound of Music* and *The Wizard of Oz* in a chapter designated for shows with large casts for children (173–190), *The Fantasticks* in a chapter about musicals that do not require sophisticated production values (291–304), and *A Funny Thing Happened on the Way to the Forum* in a chapter about musicals that do not require sophisticated choreography (125–136). *Godspell* is in a chapter about post–Golden Age musicals (primarily using rock or folk musical styles), titled "Can You Use Any Money Today?" in which he discusses musicals that are reliable sources of income (31–58). The organization of Filichia's text suggests that selecting musicals for school and community theater is principally a negotiation between what is technically possible and what will attract audiences. That the latter issue is primary in most "how-to" texts for school and community theater suggests that audiences of amateur theater most want to see musicals that they are already familiar with.

The first two plays listed, *The Fantasticks* and *Guys and Dolls*, are reported by AACT-member companies significantly more often than the remaining titles on the list, and their popularity can be viewed as an indication of audience expectations and community theaters' practical needs. Both are terrific shows with captivating music—reasons enough for audiences to want to see them repeatedly (myself included), particularly when they are performed well. Furthermore, *The Fantasticks* uses minimal sets and costumes, making it suited to low-budget community theaters. Nevertheless, it is also worth considering that these top two productions offer something in their stories that makes them consistent choices for community theaters across the United States. Both tell stories about heterosexual courtships, suggesting that gender relations are universal and that courtship rituals are something that everyone can relate to; and both exploit gender stereotypes—specifically, both present polarized images of female identity and suggest that women are either "low" or "high" in character and stature, either sexually loose or virtuously virginal.

Dramatics magazine documents a somewhat different high school musical theater canon, as an extension of its annual most popular plays list (which includes musicals, one-act, and full-length plays) from the reports of its member high schools. In 2004, the magazine inventoried all of the lists and published the most popular productions for high school theater in the United States and Canada from 1938 to 2004. From this list, the most popular musicals for high school theater production are (in order of popularity): *Bye Bye Birdie; Oklahoma!; Guys and Dolls; You're a Good Man, Charlie Brown; The Music Man; Fiddler on the Roof; Once Upon a Mattress; Grease; Godspell;* and *The Sound of Music.*[23]

All of these musicals have several qualities in common that make them suitable for high school production: they have large ensemble casts, strong vocal parts for men and women, and in several cases smaller roles for nonsingers. Very few have vulgar language by contemporary standards, contain material that will likely be offensive to parents or younger siblings (with the exception of *Grease*, which is often cut to make it more palatable), or challenge heteronormative assumptions about gender and sexuality. Four titles have onstage drinking written into the script: *Bye Bye Birdie, Guys and Dolls, Fiddler on the Roof,* and *Grease.* A teacher would likely need to confirm that the context of the drinking was acceptable to the principal, school board, and local community, or apply for permission to cut it from the performance (Bennett, 2001; Gonzalez, 2006). Deciding whether the context is acceptable is often determined by the age of the character, the historical period of the play, and how essential the consumption of alcohol is to the storyline of the play. For example, *Fiddler on the Roof* features an essential song and dance number, "To Life!" in a tavern in 1901 Russia. Although many of the characters in the scene are "underage" by today's standards, it would have been acceptable for them to drink alcohol in the historical moment of the play. Furthermore, cutting "To Life!" would confuse the storyline, and it is a song that audiences popularly expect and recognize as part of this show. On the other hand, the teenage characters who drink alcohol in *Grease* do so illegally, and its use of drinking and smoking are often thought of as elements that can be cut without compromising the storyline.[24]

The top three titles, *Bye Bye Birdie*, *Oklahoma!*, and *Guys and Dolls* all celebrate heterosexual courtship and present fairly sanitized images of gender and sexuality. Although *Guys and Dolls* has characters who gamble illegally, their actions are treated as a character defect and in the end, the gamblers must redeem themselves. Also somewhat problematic is the scene in which the chorus of women performs a "strip" show down to leotards. However, the scene is meant to be funny, and a director would likely have to make a careful decision about how skimpy the costumes are. Like the popular titles from the community musical theater canon, all three shows have courtship rituals that reinforce gender stereotypes and all three have a wedding or offstage marriage as part of the plot.

The lists documenting community and high school theaters in the United States overlap in two of their three most produced titles: *Guys and Dolls* and *Oklahoma!* Both are Tony-award winning shows that have seen frequent revivals on Broadway, both have songs familiar to even the most infrequent theatergoer, and both have been acknowledged by critical scholars and popular audiences alike among the best that the American musical theater stage has to offer.[25] Both musicals tell stories about American identity and American values, and both present heteronormative images of gender roles and relationships.

Guys and Dolls was first produced on Broadway in 1950 and is set in a slightly earlier period. The plot concerns two heterosexual courtships, that of Nathan Detroit and his long-suffering fiancée of fourteen years, Adelaide; and that of Sky Masterson and Salvation Army Sergeant Sarah Brown. Nathan bets fellow-gambler Sky that he cannot get Sarah to fly to Havana with him; Sky succeeds, and he and Sarah fall in love. However, Sarah rejects Sky when she learns that Nathan has used her Save-a-Soul Mission for his floating crap game while they were away. To save Sarah's mission from being closed, Sky "wins" sinners in a crap game and requires that they attend a prayer meeting. When Sarah learns that Sky, in addition to saving her mission, has protected her reputation by claiming to lose his bet to Nathan, she reconciles with him. They marry, as do Adelaide and a somewhat unhappy Nathan.

Conflicts in *Guys and Dolls* depend on normalizing assumptions about gender roles, stereotypes of women as either "loose" or virginal, and of men as characters who are "tamed" by the women they love. Many of the songs reinforce these assumptions. In "Adelaide's Lament," Adelaide sings about how a girl can "develop a cold" from waiting for a man to marry her. A chorus of men sings about how "guys" get "licked" by "dolls": "When you see a Joe/Saving half of his dough/You can bet there'll be mink in it for some doll." Of course, getting "licked" is integral to the show's happy ending; in the final moments, the ensemble sings: "When you meet a gent/Paying all kinds of rent/For a flat that could flatten the Taj Mahal/Call it sad, call it funny/But it's better than even money/That the guy's only doing it for some doll!"[26]

Oklahoma! was first produced on Broadway in 1943 and is set in 1907 in the "Indian territory" above Texas, telling a story of American history, identity, and values that centers around two heterosexual courtships: Laurey and Curly as the primary couple, and Will and Ado Annie as the secondary couple. Although they are encouraged by Aunt Eller, Laurey and Curly are shy around each other. Ado Annie is on the other hand flirtatious, and sings

"I'm just a girl who cain't say no" about the multiple men vying for her affection, though her father steps in and insists that she marry.[27] When hired hand Jud attempts to win Laurey's affection, Curly intervenes and marries her. Jud tries to kill Curly, but the fight ends with Jud's accidental death. In a short trial, Curly is found to have acted in self-defense, and the story ends with Curly and Laurey off to begin their honeymoon.

Oklahoma! celebrates characters who are surviving the challenges of America's expansion in the West through rugged individualism and a strong sense of how men and women should live their lives. Given the difficulty of life in the "new" West, it is not surprising that there is not room for a character like Jud, or for the child-like frolicking of Ado Annie. This is a story about people who have to work hard and depend on each other to survive; breaking social codes of behavior could be disastrous for the community and the chances of the territory becoming a state. *Oklahoma!* celebrates the foundations of the "American dream" and shows that part of that dream is heterosexual coupling, marriage, and family.

Both *Guys and Dolls* and *Oklahoma!* fulfill many of community and high school theater's technical needs: they have large, ensemble casts with multiple large roles; recognizable titles with familiar music to help sell tickets and recruit future participants; and integrated singing, dancing, and character work to allow performers with different talents and abilities to participate. The language used in both is generally inoffensive, with the possible exception of the historically and regionally specific dialect written into *Oklahoma!* Characters who engage in "objectionable" behavior, such as drinking, gambling, and violence, are either redeemed (Sky Masterson) or killed (Jud). Both shows celebrate American identity and values, supporting the idea that onstage and in the audience, community and high school theater are spaces of civic engagement, providing opportunities for people to feel a sense of belonging to something that is at once local, national, and universal. Finally, unsurprising given the time period in which they were written, both musicals contain normalized images of gender and sexuality, celebrate heterosexual rituals such as courtship and marriage, and reinforce some audiences' expectation that they should not be challenged to include nonheterosexual individuals in their community or worldview. However, even though both shows reinforce cultural assumptions about who is "normal" and what modes of gender performance are acceptable, when presented in a community or high school theater context, they are also opportunities for public debate about community membership and visibility, especially since their venues are historically understood as sites for civic engagement.

KNOWING YOUR AUDIENCE CAN BE PRODUCTIVE, BUT RISKY

The shared histories and contemporary practice of community and high school theater illuminate a unique relationship to audiences. Their history as sites of civic engagement complicates their frequent choices in musical theater production. When people in the audience and onstage know one another, the presentation of gender and sexuality—even as heteronormative stereotypes—poses questions to the community about who is valued, and who is visible. Furthermore, high school theater's historical role of teaching "life skills" and "effective citizenship" continues to challenge teachers in selecting material for production.

Guys and Dolls and *Oklahoma!* do not give nonnormative community members opportunities to see their own identities onstage, and in some contexts, it could seem as though the message of community and high school theater is that "good" and visible Americans fulfill heteronormative gender roles. However, Leah Cohen's documentation of the AFD's conflict over *M. Butterfly* demonstrates that although the "most popular" lists from AACT tend toward safe choices, selections across an entire season can be more diverse. The same is true for high school theater. Many "how-to" books for high school theater teachers encourage teacher-directors to take calculated risks with the support of their principal and school board, arguing that students' learning is at stake (Bennett, 2001; Gonzalez, 2006; Grote, 1997). To support teachers who might encounter resistance to risk-taking in their community, the American Alliance for Theatre and Education published "Freedom of Artistic Expression in Educational Theatre" in 1993, and freedom of expression is an issue regularly addressed in publications by the EdTA.[28]

Regardless of whether a musical is "safe" or "risky" for a given community or high school, the intimacy between actors and audience in these theaters raises the stakes for everyone involved. Even if a show seems safe, playing a certain character, singing a solo, dancing, or wearing a particular costume might represent a risk for an individual actor. Cohen argues that this aspect of community theater creates a rich actor-audience relationship, one that makes the play event (regardless of the "riskiness" of the text) an opportunity for public discourse, with its issues refracted through the lens of storytelling. By considering the humanity of characters in a play, actors and audience come to know themselves and each other in new ways:

> Even in the safest, tamest production of the most banal old chestnut, relationships and conflicts unfold in public; people must make themselves more vulnerable than the daily code prescribes. The nature of theatre is to expose, and in partaking of theatre, whether as actors, crew, or audience members, we are ourselves made vulnerable, laid bare to feelings and reactions; to some degree we become participants in a story that asks something of us. (L. Cohen, 2002, xvii–xviii)

Other researchers and teachers of high school theater have made observations similar to Cohen's (Bennett, 2001; Chapman, 2005, 2007; Gonzalez, 1999, 2006; Lazarus, 2004) and identified the development of empathy as one of the most important skills that theater can impart in the classroom, onstage, and in the audience (Gonzalez, 2006). Furthermore, the double meanings that can occur when actors and audience know each other allow for interesting moments of Brechtian distance, whether or not they were originally intended. Seeing a contemporary teenager play Adelaide in *Guys and Dolls* could illuminate the way that the performance of femininity is historically specific. Casting the popular quarterback to play Curly in *Oklahoma!* could challenge the idea that theater is an "unmasculine" cultural space in high school. Seeing anyone from a local community sing and dance on stage, when he or she has never been known to sing and dance before, has an element of risk that distances the audience from the play text but may make them feel closer to their fellow community member.

Empathy toward others can be a starting point for building better school and local communities that not only tolerate differences but that also encourage members to treat one another with kindness and care, even when they cannot agree with or understand one another. Although popular texts for community and high school musical performance capitalize on heteronormative assumptions and gender stereotypes, the production itself may potentially serve as a medium for inclusion and as an opportunity for public dialogue (van de Water and Giannini, 2008). The moments of intimacy when actors and/or audience share a commitment to a theater, production, story, and/or performance can be delicate sparks of shared humanity that set a foundation for expanding who is visible and knowable in communities and schools.

NOTES

1. See Louise Burleigh, *The Community Theatre in Theory and Practice* (Boston: Little, Brown, 1917); Leah Hager Cohen, *The Stuff of Dreams: Behind the Scenes of an American Community Theatre* (New York: Viking Penguin, 2001); Samuel J. Hume and Lois M. Foster, *Theatre and School* (New York: Samuel French, 1932); Lois Law, "Training in Citizenship through Play-Production" (*High School Thespian* 8.2 [October 1936]: 5, 16); and Joan Lazarus, *Signs of Change: New Directions in Secondary Theatre Education* (Portsmouth, NH: Heinemann, 2004).

2. See Sara Brady's review of Leah Hager Cohen's *The Stuff of Dreams: Behind the Scenes of an American Community Theatre* (*Drama Review* 46.1 [Spring 2002]: 170–74), and L. Cohen.

3. See L. Cohen; and Kenneth Macgowan, *The Theatre of Tomorrow* (New York: Boni and Liveright, 1921) and "Drama's New Domain—The High School" (*Harper's* [November 1929]: 774–79). For discussions of the dissemination of pre-professional knowledge and training in high school, see Tammy La Gorce, "High School Musical Actors Envision Being Rising Stars" (*New York Times*, March 15, 2009, http://www.nytimes.com/2009/03/15/nyregion/new-jersey/15papernj.html, accessed May 9, 2011), "At Home on the Stage" (*New York Times*, April 5, 2009, http://www.nytimes.com/2009/04/05/nyregion/new-jersey/05paper.html, accessed May 9, 2011), and "The Rising Star Awards: Singing! Dancing! Scholarships!" (*New York Times*, June 28, 2009, http://www.nytimes.com/2009/06/28/nyregion/28papernj.html, accessed May 9, 2011).

4. See L. Cohen; Robert E. Gard and Gertrude Burley, *Community Theatre: Idea and Achievement* (New York: Duell, Sloan, and Pearce, 1959); Jo Beth Gonzalez, *Temporary Stages: Departing from Tradition in High School Theatre Education* (Portsmouth, NH: Heinemann, 2006); Lazarus; Macgowan, 1921, 1929; and Manon van de Water and Annie Giannini, "Gay and Lesbian Theatre for Young People, or the Representation of 'Troubled Youth,'" in *We Will Be Citizens: New Essays on Gay and Lesbian Theatre*, ed. James Fisher (Jefferson, NC: McFarland, 2008), pp. 103–22.

Other amateur theater forms, such as college/university theaters and Gilbert and Sullivan societies, have also been instrumental in a grassroots dissemination of musical theater knowledge and experience. Although deserving of further attention, neither of these is considered at length in this chapter. For more information about Gilbert and Sullivan societies in and outside of the United States, see "The Gilbert and Sullivan Archive" at http://diamond. boisestate.edu/gas/, accessed September 8, 2009.

5. For exceptions see Cynthia Lynn Brown, "Longevity and the Secondary Theatre Arts Teacher: A Case Study" (Ph.D. dissertation, Arizona State University, 1997); Gonzalez, 1999, 2006; L. Cohen; Sonja Kuftinec, "A Cornerstone for Rethinking Community Theatre" (*Theatre Topics* 6.1 [March 1996]: 91–104), and "Staging the City with the Good People of New Haven" (*Theatre Journal* 53.2 [May 2001]: 197–222); Lazarus; Karlyn Love, "A Directorial Approach for a High School Production of *You Can't Take It with You* by Moss Hart and George S. Kaufman: Performed February 1, 2, 3, 2001 at Oregon City High School, Oregon City, Oregon" (M.F.A. thesis, University of Portland, 2001); Joe Norris, Laura A. McCammon, and Carole S. Miller, *Learning to Teach Drama: A Case Narrative Approach* (Portsmouth, NH: Heinemann, 2000); Carson Rothrock, "Our Own Junior High School Musical" (*English Journal* 61.8 [November 1972]: 1244–46); and Sharona Rozmaryn, "Producing a High School Production of Agatha Christie's *Ten Little Indians*: A Case Study" (Master's thesis, University of Maryland, 1994).

6. Select examples include Raina S. Ames, *A High School Theatre Teacher's Survival Guide* (New York: Routledge, 2005); Jeff Bennett, *Secondary Stages: Revitalizing High School Theatre* (Portsmouth, NH: Heinemann, 2001); Gary P. Cohen, *The Community Theater Handbook: A Complete Guide to Organizing and Running a Community Theater* (Portsmouth, NH: Heinemann, 2003); Jean Dalrymple, *The Complete Handbook for Community Theatre: From Picking Plays to Taking the Bows* (New York: Drake, 1977); Peter Filichia, *Let's Put on a Musical! How to Choose the Right Show for Your Theater*, 2nd ed. (New York: Back Stage Books, 2007); Edwin Gross and Natalie Gross, *Teen Theatre* (New York: McGraw Hill, 1953); David Grote, *Play Directing in the School: A Drama Director's*

Survival Guide (Colorado Springs, CO: Meriwether, 1997); Toby Heathcotte, *Program Building: A Practical Guide for High School Speech and Drama Teachers* (Glendale, AZ: Mardale Books, 2003); Hume and Foster; Margaret F. Johnson, *The Drama Teacher's Survival Guide: A Complete Tool Kit for Theatre Arts* (Colorado Springs, CO: Meriwether, 2007); Charlotte Kay Motter, *Theatre in High School: Planning, Teaching, Directing* (Lanham, MD: University Press of America, 1984); James Opelt, *Organizing and Managing the High School Theatre Program* (Boston: Allyn and Bacon, 1991); Jim Patterson, Donna McKenna-Crook, and Melissa Swick, *Theatre in the Secondary Classroom: Methods and Strategies for the Beginning Teacher* (Portsmouth, NH: Heinemann, 2006); William J. Rappel and John R. Winnie, *Community Theatre Handbook* (Iowa City, IA: Institute of Public Affairs, 1961); Lawrence Stern, *School and Community Theater Management: A Handbook for Survival* (Boston: Allyn and Bacon, 1979); Elizabeth Swados, *At Play: Teaching Teenagers Theater* (New York: Faber and Faber, 2006); Joy Verley, *An Essential Manual for High-School Theater Directors: How to Structure and Organize a Youth Theater Program* (Hanover, NH: Smith and Kraus, 2001); and John Wray Young, *Community Theatre: A Manual for Success* (New York: Samuel French, 1971).

7. *Millennium Theatres: Discovering Community Theatre's Future by Exploring Its Past*, ed. Shirley Harbin, Jennifer Roberts, Noelia Saenz, and Carl P. Grant (Detroit: Theatre USA, the American Association of Community Theatre, and the City of Detroit Department of Recreation, Empowerment Zone, 2004); also published online at http://www.aact.org/aact/Millennium_Theatres2b.pdf, accessed September 10, 2009.

8. Hume and Foster; Macgowan, 1921, 1929. For a contemporary look at this issue in schools, see Laurie Fox, "Staging *Phantom* an Epic Task for Southlake Carroll" (*Dallas Morning News*, December 8, 2007, http://www.dentonrc.com/sharedcontent/dws/dn/latestnews/stories/120907dnmetphantom.4deb77.html, accessed May 9, 2011), and "Carroll Senior High Stages *Phantom of the Opera*" (*Dallas Morning News*, December 9, 2007, http://www.quickdfw.com/sharedcontent/dws/news/localnews/stories/DN-phantom_09met.ART.State.Edition2.3706394.html, accessed May 9, 2011.

9. For further information about the little theater movement, see Dorothy Chansky, *Composing Ourselves: The Little Theatre Movement and the American Audience* (Carbondale: Southern Illinois University Press, 2004); see also Burleigh; and Oscar G. Brockett and Franklin J. Hildy, *History of the Theatre*, 9th ed. (New York: Allyn and Bacon, 2003), pp. 457–58.

10. See Jennifer Chapman, "Heteronormativity and High School Theatre" (Ph.D. dissertation, University of Wisconsin-Madison, 2005) and "Heteronormativity and High School Theatre" (*Youth Theatre Journal* 21 [2007]: 31–40); see also Macgowan, 1921, 1929.

11. Edward A. Krug, *The Shaping of the American High School: 1920–1941* (Madison: University of Wisconsin Press, 1972), especially pp. 20–25.

12. See Earl W. Blank, "Why Boys Should Study Dramatics" (*High School Thespian* VIII [September/October 1936]: 6; 15–16); Lois Law, "Training in Citizenship Through Play Production" (*High School Thespian* VIII [November/December 1936]: 5, 16); Louise J. Lovett, "Dramatics in Negro High Schools" (*High School Thespian* VII [March/April 1936]: 9, 13).

13. "Membership Roll of the National Thespians" (*High School Thespian* 1 [October 1929]: 54); "National Thespian Roll" (*High School Thespian* 10.5 [May/June 1939]: 51).

14. American Association of Community Theatres (http://www.aact.org, accessed September 10, 2009).

15. "Dedication" (*Dramatics* 22 [January 1951]: 1); the uncited quotation is from Alexander Pope's "Essay on Man," Epistle IV.

16. American Educational Theatre Association, "Course of Study Materials for a High School Dramatics Course" (*Bulletin of the National Association of Secondary-School Principals* [December 1949]: 5–7, 23–25).

17. Educational Theatre Association, "Writer's Guidelines" (http://www.edta.org/pdf_archive/dramatics_writers_guide.pdf, accessed September 11, 2009).

18. See the U.S. Department of Education Web site (http://www.ed.gov/policy/elsec/leg/esea02/index.html, accessed September 11, 2009) for the full text of the No Child Left Behind Act, reauthorized in 2001.

19. See Burleigh; Heather Cousins, "Upholding Mainstream Culture: The Tradition of the American High School Play" (*Research in Drama Education* 5.1 [2000]: 85–94); Hume and Foster; Law; and Macgowan 1921.

20. Wilhelmina P. Brown, "Hints for the High School Director" (*Dramatics* 19.1 [September 1947]: 12–13).

21. These needs are also met by Gilbert and Sullivan operettas. However, a school with a sophisticated dance department (or with student dancers who train at a local studio) might find the choreography in these alternative "safe" choices somewhat bland because of their dependence on a double chorus.

22. For examples of how students, schools, and communities struggle over redefining what is "appropriate" for teenagers in high school theater, see Jeff Overly, "Instructor: Play Canceled Because of Gay Character" (*Orange County Register*, February 13, 2009, http://articles.ocregister.com/2009–02–13/cities/24657324_1_gay-characters-gay-and-lesbian-students-drama-teacher, accessed May 9, 2011); and Patrick Healy, "Tamer *Rent* Is Too Wild for Some Schools" (*New York Times*, February 20, 2009, http://www.nytimes.com/2009/02/20/arts/20iht-20rent.20328998.html?pagewanted=1&%2339&%2359;t%20Look%2040,%20Charlie%20Brown!&sq=You%20Don&st=Search&scp=4, accessed May 9, 2011).

23. Educational Theatre Association, "The Long Run" (*Dramatics* 76 [September 2004]: 19–20).

24. Bennett points out that there are other objectionable qualities about *Grease* that make it inappropriate for high school students, namely, its sexism and sentimentalizing of high school. For more discussion of this issue, see also Michael Criscuolo's online review of *Grease* from August 22, 2007 (http://www.nytheatre.com/nytheatre/showpage.php?t=grea5104, accessed September 12, 2009).

25. For example, see John Lahr, "Broadway Boogie-Woogie" (*New Yorker*, March 9, 2009: 78).

26. Quoted lyrics are from act I, scenes iv and v, and act II, scene vii; Frank Loesser, Jo Swerling, Abe Burrows, and Damon Runyon, *Guys and Dolls: A Musical Fable of Broadway* (London: Frank Music, 1951).

27. Quoted lyric is from act II, scene ii; Richard Rodgers and Oscar Hammerstein II, *Oklahoma!* (New York: Williamson Music, 1943).
28. American Alliance for Theatre and Education, "Freedom of Artistic Expression in Educational Theatre" (*Drama Theatre Teacher* 5.3 [1993]: A1–A3).

9

Performance, Authenticity, and the Reflexive Idealism of the American Musical

RAYMOND KNAPP

■ □ ■

THE AMERICAN MUSICAL, THROUGHOUT ITS history, has proved capable of reinventing itself in countless, often unexpected ways.[1] In this capacity, it has mirrored one of its own dominant themes, allied closely to its most distinctive performance modes, singing and dancing. That theme is a kind of reflexive idealism, based on the implicit belief that renewal and redemption are always possible, that people can and should reinvent themselves as necessary, and in the process discover and unlock unexplored capabilities and capacities. In this final chapter of the volume, I first consider one of the negative dimensions of this thematic emphasis, which has placed the musical at odds with modes of musical authenticity long dominant in critical discourses. I then explore how reflexive idealism, as a transformative meta-theme, plays out both in performance generally and in the specific contexts of *Candide* and *Man of La Mancha*. Key to both prongs of my discussion is a transgressive dimension of performance especially evident in musicals, encapsulated in the carelessly affirmative response musicals give to the rather serious question, "Can either authenticity or idealism be advanced through the blatantly artificial modes of performance offered up in musicals?"

PERFORMING AUTHENTICITY

The musical has long provided fertile soil for American popular music, producing hit songs and jazz standards; fostering the song traditions of Tin Pan Alley; and accommodating elements of ragtime, jazz, blues, and other emergent popular styles. Yet the musical, while mostly ignored by those who work the "serious" side of the musicology and theater streets, is similarly marginalized within the burgeoning field of popular music studies. Within that realm, musicals belong to a large body of music—including Barry Manilow, disco, the Eagles, smooth jazz, Celine Dion, and so on—that, although manifestly popular, has been traditionally ignored or treated with disdain, amusement, or embarrassment.[2]

The reasons for this are many, but let's start with some history. The study of popular music arose in earnest during the long shadow of the 1960s and has ever since tended to reflect important issues and attitudes from that era, in many cases directly carried over from such periodicals as *Rolling Stone* or the *Village Voice*. To traverse some of that landscape: Youthful rebellion and the counterculture were establishing and reinforcing the boundaries of the generation gap. The civil rights movement and evolving notions of racial identity in America became politically energizing issues for the younger side of that gap. The sexual revolution was in full swing. The mainstream study of classical music was still ideologically opposed to serious engagement with the cultural and political foundations of music. The boundaries between American musicology and ethnomusicology were increasingly fluid regarding American music. And, enforcing and coloring the interactions of this potent mix of issues, attitudes, and circumstances, music's capacity to instill emotional fervor made questions of authenticity and relevance seem especially important.

Within this environment, two narratives of authenticity attached to popular music with particular force. Jazz and blues became seen as the foundational music of African Americans as a people, establishing along with spirituals a heritage that authenticated their claims to depth, emotional capacity, and cultural legitimacy during a time when that was at issue. And for many who were then coming of age, rock-and-roll emerged as an offshoot of blues and country, rapidly becoming the principal vehicle of youthful musical expression by offering sexualized, politicized, and directly *real* expressions of rock musicians' subjectivity, powerful enough to weld together a collection of causes, complaints, and compulsions into the semblance of a movement. Supporting these narratives was a centuries-old tendency to find musical authenticity among the working and peasant classes, which translated, in American terms, into whatever might be understood as "roots" music, especially when it expressed real or imagined experiences of victimhood.[3]

It is easy to see why Barry Manilow and the musical would seem just as irrelevant to all this as classical music. The area of popular music studies, especially as it tried to secure a foothold in the academy, engaged not so much with popularity, nor even with music per se, but rather with types of music within popular culture that seemed capable of engaging its broadly based, activist narratives.[4] Music that offered comfort, enforced the status quo, or gestured too strongly toward older mainstreams

simply did not count, however popular or musically interesting. As for the *musical* study of musicals, it tended to retain the perspectives, methodologies, and borrowed prestige of
traditional musicology, where it had long shared a ghetto with
popular music more generally.

But why should a criterion such as "authenticity"—so obvi-
ously problematic and, well, *phony*—have the capacity to carry
rock and jazz into academic legitimacy while so many other
musical styles and practices languish in their various mixes of
real-world popularity and academic obscurity? The answer has
to do with a somewhat older academic history, that of musicology itself.

Musicology became established as a discipline during the
nineteenth century in part as an outgrowth of German Idealism
and German nationalism, which gave a direction and purpose
to the young discipline: to foster a canon of serious, mainly
German, musical works. The overriding standard of value was
set by German Idealism, with its dual focus on subjectivity
and the Infinite, and its ongoing difficulties regarding the real
world. As German Idealism took hold, music became seen as
the highest of the arts, capable of linking intense subjectivity
directly to something much larger, be it nation, the world in
some deep sense, or something beyond the world, such as God,
universal consciousness, or the Will. These larger somethings
were mostly interchangeable as far as music was concerned,
allowing it to accommodate easily to the evolving constructs of
German Idealism. But the focus on the musical *subject* as the
generator of musical value—of music as such—and, from the
other side, on music as the purest expression of subjectivity, became the foundation of a new understanding of music that has
ever since dominated discourses on musical value.

Within popular music studies, the cult of authenticity stems
directly from this historically based valorization of subjective
musical expression, and links up to both a related valorization

of folk music as authentic within nationalist discourses and a strong latter-day emphasis on the recapturing of origins, whether in source studies, sketch studies, editions, or performance practice. All of these seek authenticity by reaching back to moments of inspiration or conception, of first thoughts and first performances or modes of performance, in order to bring us as close as possible to the unmediated expression of the originating subject or subjects.

In contrast with the hard-won authenticities of the classical canon and the projected authenticities of jazz and rock, musicals offer instead a multi-authored, highly collaborative, eclectic, star-driven commercial product in which roles are performed in the most artificial of modes: the glitzy glitter of song and dance, often with an admixture of camp. And these products are sustained not by artists steeped in a revered tradition but by a full gamut of performers, from Broadway casts performing the same routines every night, to musical neophytes lip-synching to playback that may or may not include their own voices, kids in high schools, college and community groups, and really, anyone who might want to sing or dance along to a cast album. How much further from the paradigms of authenticity could you get?

To illustrate how deep the divide between these worlds has been, historically, we might consider *Bye Bye Birdie* (1960), a show that addresses many of the issues I've identified, but especially the generation gap and the supposed authenticity of rock-and-roll. The show's parodic dismissal of the latter, welcomed by critics of the time, in retrospect seems a bit clueless, as if the show has not taken the full measure of what it parodies. This has partly to do with its timing; the show played between 1960 and 1961, when rock-and-roll seemed to have run its course, just before its dramatic resurgence and reification as rock. And this has partly to do with the unidimensionality of the show's faux-rock-and-roll songs, "Honestly Sincere" and "One

Last Kiss," both of which devolve into excessive repetitions of simple-minded lyrics. Within songs that are fundamentally Golden Age Broadway layered with elements of rock-and-roll, this blatant repetition points in two directions at once: to the banality of directly expressed feeling as such, however authentic or "sincere," and to the vain pretensions of Conrad Birdie— the show's manipulated rock-and-roll icon, modeled on Elvis Presley—whose authenticity is clearly a pose (⬤ Example 9.1; ⬤ Example 9.2).[5]

These song parodies have not worn well on film or in revival, where they serve mainly as vehicles for slightly exaggerated rock-and-roll performances. In a sense, the rock-and-roll ethos itself rejects their parodic dimension, absorbing it into a mode of authenticating abjection, and so making their sharper barbs seem gratuitous. More basically, the parody of these songs fails because it takes rock-and-roll's claims to authenticity as the central issue, instead of querying how such claims *function* for those who invest in them. But to get at this dimension, we must indulge in some historical speculation.

Claims of authenticity regarding rock-and-roll began when teenagers who had become hooked on it in the '50s became adults and didn't want to let it go. To rationalize this desire, college students and other young adults developed what might be called a rhetoric of relevance, through which they attached this music directly to things that mattered, at least to them: to youthful idealism; or to forms of political and social protest, especially as they involved race, war, and sexual freedom. In the process, "rock-and-roll" became "rock," and there were four compelling reasons for the shift in terminology. Aesthetically, the shorter term seemed purer and more powerful, as if condensing rock-and-roll to its essence. Moreover, it freed this music from its function as dance music, foregrounding instead its capacity either to *em*power or to *over*power, and so to inspire a different kind of movement. And the new term made it seem as if the style itself were somehow elemental, obscuring its origins as a hybrid style. But more practically and decisively, rock became a term used in combination with other musical terms—as with folk-rock, an initially controversial fusion in which rock lent its power to a proven musical vehicle of political protest. Whether in combination or in one of its increasingly varied forms, rock thus became the basic music currency of the counterculture.

Which makes it particularly interesting to notice, regarding *Bye Bye Birdie*, not only its setting just *before* all this gets under way but also its near elimination of the college-age generation. It has teenagers and adults in large number, and a sprinkling of pre-teens who either feel left out or form alliances with the adults. But there are no college-age young adults to speak of—except for the show's leads. Albert and Rose are aging members of this cohort, fending off both generations at once, caught for eight years—that is, since around 1950—between the oppressive caricature of Albert's mother and, at least for part of that span, the callowness of Conrad Birdie. In the end, their dramatic project is to free themselves from both sides.

But anyone who's ever been involved with *Bye Bye Birdie* in repertory knows that for a significant swath of the cast and audience, the star of the show is neither Albert nor Rose, but Conrad. Conrad is, after all, more precisely part of the pivotal age group than either Albert or Rose, and he has the rapt attention of those who are at stake, especially Kim MacAfee, who—at least by aspiration—is coming of age when the show opens. But the issue is even more basic than that: how can Elvis—even a parody of Elvis—be *in* the show and not be its *star*?

And this gets directly to the heart of the problem: from the perspective of the preemptive authenticity of the rock aesthetic as it evolved in the years immediately following the show's run, Conrad—even as a parody—trumps the musical's core plot, no matter how extravagantly decked out with elements borrowed from *West Side Story, Gypsy,* and other shows from the recent past, and no matter that the show is basically right about role-playing in the rock-and-roll scene of the late '50s. Even if the bigger project in mounting *Bye Bye Birdie* is to put on a musical, you're also putting on a rock concert, and it's hard to keep the show's focus centered on Albert and Rose when most of the cast is modeling fandom directed elsewhere, whether to Conrad Birdie or to Ed Sullivan.

While this may seem to place musicals and "authenticity" at an impasse, there is, crucially, a dimension of German Idealism (and its American offshoots)[6] that I've sidestepped by focusing on the category of authenticity as it is generally understood (usually implicitly) in popular music studies. German Idealism is not about indulging the subjective position above all else but rather about the imperative to develop one's self so as to align with larger forces. It thus came to underwrite the German concept of *Bildung,* a term taken over in the late eighteenth century from Pietism, pointing to a deepened sense of education that encompasses character formation and the capacities for reflection and realizing individual potential. To the extent that ideals of authenticity seek to reify the presentation of self within some frozen, essentialized state, indulging one's feelings over one's potential, they are not based in German Idealism, but in a self-indulgent tributary. The core of German Idealism is about *change.*

Now, this is not *in*consistent with many elements of rock, which strikes a balance between the impulse to support either protest or progressive agendas, and the tendency to hold fast to particular modes of expression, which might be rendered impure if allowed to evolve and cross-breed with other modes of expression. But this transformative mode of authenticity is more fully and fundamentally consistent with the musical. As theater, the musical is about enacting change, and it is no coincidence that one of its most time-honored devices has been the transformation scene. In this, it plays not so much to German Idealism (with its aversion to transcendence) as to a characteristic American optimism, to beliefs about realizing potential and the capacity for redemption, or for responding to disaster by starting afresh. Corollary to this, musicals also do two other things: they involve music as a kind of fluid medium that facilitates change (and allows us to believe in it); and they also typically involve a dramatically delineated process of *earning* the desired change, through performance. These processes are part and parcel of how musicals work: characters have something to learn, and music teaches them what they need to know—including their capacity to learn it—while at the same time providing an environment that facilitates change. And except for the distraction of Conrad Birdie's insincere sincerities, *Bye Bye Birdie*, like most musicals, strives to work in precisely this way, especially with regard to Rose and Albert.

Further examples are legion: Magnolia in *Show Boat*, who early on is too enamored of appearances but learns to find and express shared truths through performance. Curly and Laurey in *Oklahoma!*, who early on *don't* learn enough from their shared songs, and emerge as a successful couple only by aligning—through song—with larger forces. Fred and Lilli in *Kiss Me, Kate*, who learn to perform themselves and their relationship through the characters they perform on stage, in song. Anna in *The King and I*, who teaches through both song and dance but also learns (most importantly, about herself) through performing the role of teacher. Most of the cast of *The Music Man*, who align with community through music. And Maria in *The Sound of Music*, who does it all: teaching through song, gaining courage through performance (at least in the film version), and, most extraordinary of all for a star on Broadway, attending quietly while someone else teaches her how one builds one's own character, in "Climb Ev'ry Mountain," the quintessential *Bildung* song.

In musicals, transformation, self-discovery, and self-expression all happen through performance. One may well argue that Broadway stars aren't really performing *themselves* but are instead performing *roles*.[7] But in truth, as I will explore more broadly in the following section, they *are* performing themselves, or at least that part of themselves that can be forged through performance. In merging their public personae with the roles they play on stage, stars demonstrate that one may perform selfhood much like any other role, internalizing it but directing it outward into specific action—a mode of performance perfectly in line with dramatic, vocal, and danced performance more generally. Musicals matter to people largely because they provide fluid musical texts that inscribe possibilities of social interaction and change, first observed in performance but then taken over through processes of internal modeling or external reenactment, which allows people to discover aspects of who they are, and (re)imagine who they might become.

PERFORMING IDEALISM

Because the musical is a highly collaborative, commercial art form involving both drama and music, its intertwining of creation and performance, on all levels, is distinctively rich. The so-called creative team—lyricist, librettist, composer, arranger, choreographer, director, set, lighting, and costume designers—all play to an audience as much, if less directly, as those on stage and in the pit. And the familiar claim that original cast members "create" their roles is not as grandiose as it sounds; indeed, in a literally vital sense all stage performers create their roles—bringing them to life through their own performing bodies and projected personae—even if they follow models, obey their directors, and adhere closely to their given texts. On a still broader level, *all* of the above are involved in a process of performance-based *re*-creation, contributing to a performed re-creation of the genre itself with every new mounting of a show, re-inscribing or overturning the practices and tropes of musicals on all levels.

Understood this way, interpretation and re-creation always already inform every facet of putting on a musical, combining to create a complex layering of performances at every stage. To perform a given role convincingly, an actor must make that role his or her own, merging identities as a performer and human being with those of an interpreted text. In situations that involve the mediating step of adaptation, this process of assimilation— sometimes devolving into a kind of performer-based imperi- alism of the present over the past—involves another layered stage. Authors who base a musical on a literary text are also in this sense performers, bringing to life the literary basis they are setting, adjusting it, whether consciously or unconsciously, to fit contemporary circumstances and their stars' capacities, and thereby creating a new text as a basis for performance in the more conventional sense. Nor does the layering stop there, since audience members (or auditors of recordings) quite often appropriate these performances, making them their own in various ways, by re-performing them or by performing their lives alongside, harnessing their rhythms, sentiments, and affects to their own purposes. Thus, they may sing the songs of a musical in the shower; sing along or lip-synch with the original cast recording on their phonograph, CD player, or iPod; or borrow energy by listening to show songs as they walk, drive, Web-surf, or perform other tasks. At each stage within this layered process of remaking and performance, identities are conceived and reconceived, formed and re-formed, and, above all, *per*formed, which is a matter of both assimilation and self-invention.[8]

Useful to consider alongside this performance-based dimension, and in extension, is the specific comic tone of the American musical, including camp, which persists even within musicals on serious subjects and both depends on and helps support the resolute belief, often presented as a specifically American attitude, that a "cockeyed optimism" is an appropriate response to adversity. We may think of this as the "happy-ending" expectation of musical comedy (and comedy more generally). Humor in American musicals tends to suggest that negative forces need not be taken seriously, or at least should not be allowed the final say, an attitude that emerges as a particularly American form of idealism. These two intertwined elements of the American musical—its performed re-creations on several layered levels and its comic tone—are largely responsible for what I term its reflexive idealism.

In the remainder of this chapter, I consider, in demonstration of this dual basis, the reflexive idealism that directs the hopeful narratives of the musicals based on Cervantes's two-volume novel *Don Quixote* (1605 and 1615) and Voltaire's novella *Candide* (1759). Each of these source texts is vehemently anti-idealist, opposing a brand of idealism popular in its day—*Don Quixote* the persistence of a nostalgic longing for the age of chivalry, and *Candide* the optimism associated with the Enlightenment. Both texts' protagonists repeatedly survive extreme physical violence, humiliation, and deprivation, appearing more and more ridiculous as they persist in beliefs that run counter to the worlds they live in—worlds not so different from those of Voltaire's and Cervantes's first readers. And both were adapted for the musical stage during the final decade of Broadway's "Golden Age," *Candide* in 1956 and *Man of La Mancha* in 1965.

Despite the anti-idealism of their sources, both musicals are strongly idealist, and in three important ways. First, as with many Broadway shows during this period, *Candide* and *Man of La Mancha* reflect a desire to elevate the American musical by drawing upon venerated texts. This is, to be sure, the idealism of middle-brow culture, but it is firmly grounded in the optimism of eighteenth-century Enlightenment beliefs and aspirations—the very target of Voltaire's *Candide*, with its unbroken parade of human misery. This type of idealism, however, sometimes comes into direct conflict with a second type of idealism fundamental to musicals, as noted: their apparently reflexive impulse to instill hope and optimism, even when neither seems warranted. I explore this second idealist mode before introducing the third.

The reflexive idealism of the American musical has a specifically musical basis, relating to its comic tone and deriving from European musical comedy in the eighteenth century—borrowing in particular the sanguine assurances of tonality, the sustaining musical achievement of the eighteenth century. The familiar tautologies of tonality—embedded in its syntax and realized within a wide variety of new forms—carry with them the assurance that things will work out, that we will find our way home. Every single time, no matter what. True, those tautologies could be put to other expressive and narrative uses—for example, through irony, or through enforcing the sense that we cannot escape our given situations, however inhospitable, so that we *must* return home whether we want to or not. Thus, irony and fate-based tropes, among other archetypes, find ready expression in tonality. But the fundamental and most often exploited affect of tonality, at least on the popular musical stage, then as now, is a basic cheerfulness founded in optimism, even if that cheerfulness can, in its very ubiquity, seem insincere or jaded at times.[9]

In illustration, we may consider *West Side Story* and *The Music Man*, which opened in 1957, the year after the original short run of *Candide*. *West Side Story*—based like *Candide* on a venerated literary property—is a tragedy, yet it clings to the fundamental optimism that sustains the reflexive idealism of the American musical stage. It performs Shakespeare's *Romeo and Juliet* by grounding tragedy in contemporary gang violence, reinforced with a gritty urbanized musical syntax based in jazz, serialism, and other contemporary idioms. But it also performs its audience's need to experience hope, allowing its Juliet to live and ending with a reprise of the most hopeful music of the show, "Somewhere." Moreover, the extended audience for *West Side Story* has tended to perform an even more hopeful version of the show, displacing its tragedy with either its core of redeeming love—by singing "Maria"—or a more hopeful version of the future than the show itself allows, by singing "Tonight" without its counterpoint of incipient violence and sexual craving (sung in the show by the rival gangs and Anita, respectively). Even so, *West Side Story* initially proved less successful than *The Music Man*, a show that promotes its musical fantasies as a cure for all social problems and ultimately insists on the reality of its alternative world, asserting, essentially, that to lie to the accompaniment of music—even music as only *imagined*, through the "think system"—is to tell the truth.

This kind of ontological assertion is the mainstay of the American musical, which presents its fantasies as alternative realities, ultimately more important than whatever more conventional reality is being displaced. But the assertion is conditional; one must experience that music as true for its reality to emerge; which means, one must in some sense *perform* it, if only internally. In this way, the American musical is habitually both idealist and optimistically realist, creating an analogue of the idealist interior world through its capacity to project fantasy and providing the material for performing a version of those fantasies in the real world.

Candide initially fared poorly in this environment, its ironies buried beneath a heavy-handed book, its music pared back to bubbles and mirth, and its audience left wondering how to reconcile what the show's book was saying with what the music seemed to be saying. The subsequent history of the show has been about following the music, which is more immediate and richer than the original book, long since replaced. With the cult-based success of the original cast album as inspiration, the concert-repertory status of the overture as standard bearer, and a treasure trove of previously discarded music as fuel, the show was gradually developed from an uneasy operetta into the semblance of an opera, a culmination of sorts for the aspirational idealism that originally fueled the project.[10] The specific contribution of the music, both to the original failure and to the later success of the project, thus warrants some scrutiny.

To begin with, the overture flat-out lies to us about what to expect. Reasonably enough, it uses the two opening numbers as they were then—"The Best of All Possible Worlds" and "Oh, Happy We"—as the basis for a foreshortened "sonata form." Sonata form—the crowning achievement of eighteenth-century tonality—provides a structure for presenting and resolving conflicts that can be represented as contrasting themes, initially presenting those themes in contrasting keys, but eventually playing the second of them in the key of the first. From this structure, we know (or think we know) that everything will work out (🔊 Example 9.3). To be sure, the overture also tells us other important information: that it won't be easy; that it will involve carnivalesque exaggeration; and that the ending may not be quite as expected, since the resolution of the "love" theme does not bring the overture to a close but yields instead to a fast coda based on a later number from the show ("Glitter and Be Gay"). In its very mastery of tradition, form, and material, the overture reassures us, encouraging us to believe that the world we are about to enter, though a bit out of kilter, is "the best of all possible worlds"—a sentiment that the show in all its versions, like Voltaire's novella, turns squarely on its ear. And perhaps, so does the overture, by topping its innocent love theme with the cynical laughter of "Glitter and Be Gay"—in which case it is still lying, in pretending not to care about the innocence it mocks (Example 9.4).

Candide's music also offers, as counterweight to this mix of idealism and mockery, a persuasive idealist trajectory set across the show, much of which has been restored only with the 1989 "opera" version. This trajectory records the protagonist's journey from idealism through disillusionment to wisdom, in a series of meditations framed by chorales in the style of Bach (Example 9.5; Example 9.6; Example 9.7). The first chorale sets the text, "We have learned, and understood/Everything that is, is good" (Example 9.8; Example 9.9), and the final one concludes with "Life is neither good nor bad./Life is life, and all we know" (Example 9.10), setting up the final number, "Make Our Garden Grow," with its sober commitment to life and work. That final number convinces in part because of its musical lineage from the meditations and chorales, but even more it depends on a single masterstroke within the closing section, when the orchestra falls away suddenly, leaving the choir to continue on its own. The gesture invokes traditions of a cappella singing as an emblem of community but also depends on the visceral effect of removing all external foundations from the singers, who must then do their best without help, a musical correlative for their dramatic situation. In this moment, the cast stands before us suddenly exposed, and the thorny counterpoint ensures that we hear them struggle a bit before they emerge together on the culminating phrase, "And make our garden grow" (Example 9.11).

Yet, however well realized this core musical elaboration of *Candide*'s redemptive theme may be, it still matters that the overture has lied to us, because the overture and much of *Candide*'s music more generally (especially the cast album selections) indelibly imprint a world in which innocence somehow *can* be preserved through it all. Voltaire knew better.

And so surely did Bernstein—why else would he have so carefully nurtured a musical narrative that entails the complete *disillusionment* of Candide's opening innocence? But despite this knowledge, the show's music, perhaps generically, tries to have it both ways.

Emblematic of the show's affective divergence from Voltaire's novella is the matter of Cunegonde's appearance at the end of the show. On Broadway and the opera stage she remains enduringly youthful and beautiful even then, but Voltaire renders her, more realistically, as having grown old and ugly before her time. Cunegonde's appearance as an operetta ingénue seems "naturally" to preempt the aging process, underscoring the music's assertion of unspoiled innocence, but there is another idealist mode at work—the third of my promised three—which offers a fuller explanation for this particular divergence.

Typically in musicals of this era, major themes are elaborated within coupled heterosexual relationships, as a way of making those themes directly performable.[11] In a musical that makes idealism its central theme, the central relationship will most often be a problematic or unsuccessful love story, serving as a "reality check" on the ability of the idealistic hero to realize his ideals; in one way or another, the idealized woman, who stands symbolically for the idealist dimension of the show, fails to live up to the demands of that symbolic function. A musical may thus bring dramatic emphasis to bear on idealist potentials, arguing through plotting and musical numbers that ideals are more valuable than their potential for realization and matter beyond the realities that prevent their fulfillment. According to this familiar trope of musicals, another lie that *Candide* indulges is that, despite the wisdom that Candide acquires, even about Cunegonde, the music itself does not admit—perhaps generically cannot admit—to Cunegonde's failures as the embodied ideal.

Man of La Mancha, on the other hand, by embracing more fully its responsibility to its time and place, emerges as more successful than *Candide*, despite the greater violence it does to its source material and despite the fact that *Candide*, for all its contradictions, is smarter, richer, and more ambitious. *Man of La Mancha* succeeds at all relevant levels of performance, in particular by speaking more directly to its contemporary audience through its hit tune, "The Impossible Dream," which became an international anthem of idealist striving.

Working backward through the three musicals-based idealist modes I've identified, we may note how much better the "ideal woman" trope works in *Man of La Mancha*, which awakens latent idealism in the brutalized Aldonza, as an emblem of the redemptive power of idealism; through her character, we see how identities might be reformed, *per*formed, and, finally, *trans*formed. Moreover, this mode extends and effectively overlaps the first idealist mode, giving dramatic presence to the "real-life" transformative potential of great literature, even if it must first be rendered accessible to the uneducated and illiterate. Through the example offered by Cervantes's fellow-prisoners, whose lives are changed by acting out his improvised account of his unfinished novel, the musical reinforces both the Aldonza-Dulcinea transformation and the larger aspirational project, of elevating the musical by drawing on great literature. Thus, in *Man of La Mancha*, these idealist modes are aligned, rather than opposed as in *Candide*.

The specifically musical idealist mode in *Man of La Mancha*, as is typical for this era, is built around the familiarity of the 32-bar Tin Pan Alley song type, which can most easily be seen in "The Impossible Dream." The song lays out the tenets of chivalry with a carefully balanced tension between internal ideals and outward action, couched in a characteristic Spanish idiom whose ostinato rhythms serve as an emblem of steadfast obsession. The song unfolds within a Tin Pan Alley form but with a "heroic" expansion of the bridge. Within this structure, the lyric at first maintains a careful alternation between inward-directed idealism and the heroic action it inspires ("To dream... To fight..."), throwing increasing emphasis to action ("To try... To reach..."; ◑ Example 9.12). Active verbs then carry us to a climax during the bridge, which dissipates in a series of idealist verbs; significantly, the verbs that mark the climax itself are idealist ("And I *know* if I'll only *be true*..."). Finally, the satisfying completion of the well-known form—the return to the melody of the first phrase, after the bridge—adds conviction to the lyric's concluding concern for legacy, for how the world itself might be transformed through the image of the inspired, idealist hero (◑ Example 9.13).

Part of what makes *Man of La Mancha* "work" better than *Candide* is the way it manages performance on every level. Whatever its strengths as a performable text, *Candide*'s move to opera has confirmed that it is more about being a text than a show; not by coincidence, it has been published, at various stages in its development, more thoroughly than any other piece of American musical theater. As a text, it promises to outlive *Man of La Mancha*. But because the latter "performed" *Don Quixote* more appropriately for its intended venue and audience; because its onstage players so vividly enact its central metatheatrical theme and are redeemed, as characters, specifically through *performing* their redemption; and because it provided one of the central anthems through which its extended audience forged and performed the idealist component of their identities, its cultural impact has been much more powerful and lasting.

A central lesson to be learned from all reflexively idealist musicals is how lasting their moments of expressed idealism are, especially when sung, far outliving the cataclysms that often surround those moments. And in performing this reflexive idealism, both *Candide* and *Man of La Mancha* are, despite all odds, true to their originals, whose protagonists—at least in reception, and whatever Cervantes or Voltaire might have intended—have provided some of the key idealist images that have sustained Europe-based culture.

I have in this chapter addressed the need for a more congenial environment, especially within musicology, for the study of musicals, and argued for a perspective more centered on performance and less beholden to inherited notions of authenticity or text-bound standards of value. There has, indeed, been a broad surge of performance-based studies of the musical in the past few years, and a similar surge in studies that place performance at the center of musicological inquiry. One can only hope, with reflexive optimism, that these waves will be sustained, and that they will grow stronger in alignment.

NOTES

1. I have presented much of this essay's argument in a series of talks: "Cervantes, Voltaire, and the Reflexive Idealism of the American Musical" ("Musical Theater and Identity in Eighteenth-Century Spain and America," symposium held at the UCLA William Andrews Clark Memorial Library, Los Angeles, October 27–28, 2006), "Performing Authenticity; or, Why the Musical Doesn't Seem to Count as Popular Music" ("American Musical Theater," conference hosted by CUNY Graduate Center, April 2–5, 2008), and "The Musical, the American Musical, and 'Musical Comedy': Reflections on the Comic Inclinations of a Genre" ("Music and Humor," conference hosted by Echo: A Music-Centered Journal, UCLA, June 5–6, 2009). My examples draw upon my discussions of *Candide* and *Man of La Mancha* in *The American Musical and the Performance of Personal Identity* (Princeton, NJ: Princeton University Press, 2006), and I further advance the main argument of this essay in *Making Light: Haydn, Musical Camp, and the Long Shadow of Musical Idealism* (Durham: Duke University Press, 2018), especially in chapter 5.

2. An important exception to this trend is Mitchell Morris's *The Persistence of Sentiment: Essays on Pop Music in the '70s* (Berkeley and Los Angeles: University of California Press, 2012), which considers several components of this list. Regarding the musical's lack of prestige, as theater, see David Savran's chapter in this volume, as well as his "Middlebrow Anxiety" (in his *A Queer Sort of Materialism: Recontextualizing American Theater* [Ann Arbor: University of Michigan Press, 2003]); and, regarding theater's intersection with jazz and the popular more generally, his *Highbrow/Lowdown: Theater, Jazz, and the Making of the New Middle Class* (Ann Arbor: University of Michigan Press, 2009); and "Toward a Historiography of the Popular" (*Theatre Survey* 45.2 [November 2004]: 211–17). See also Carl Wilson's extended discussion of *Céline Dion in Let's Talk about Love: A Journey to the End of Taste* (New York: Continuum International, 2007).

3. For a trenchant (and entertaining) account of this period, detailing its history while also querying its mythologies and what has motivated and sustained them, see Robynn Stilwell, "Music of the Youth Revolution: Rock through the 1960s," in *The Cambridge History of Twentieth-Century Music*, ed. Nicholas Cook and Anthony Pople (Cambridge: Cambridge University Press, 2004), pp. 418–52.

4. See, however, Elijah Wald's *How the Beatles Destroyed Rock 'n' Roll: An Alternative History of American Popular Music* (New York: Oxford University Press, 2009), which takes as its scholarly starting point an obligation to consider what music was actually popular at a given time, rather than what music best fits the conventional narratives of American popular music.

5. For more on the background and rock dimension of *Bye Bye Birdie*, see Elizabeth Wollman, *The Theater Will Rock: A History of the Rock Musical from Hair to Hedwig* (Ann Arbor: University of Michigan Press, 2006), pp. 16–20. Elsewhere in the book, Wollman speaks directly to the question of authenticity as a contentious category within rock musicals; see especially pp. 24–41.

6. For an extended discussion of how German Idealism relates to the idealism prevalent in American musicals, see chapter 4 of my *The American Musical and the Performance of Personal Identity*.

7. Regarding the important connections between stars' personae and the roles they play (on stage and for their audiences), see Holley Replogle-Wong's contribution to this volume, and Stacy Wolf's *A Problem Like Maria: Gender and Sexuality in the American Musical* (Ann Arbor: University of Michigan Press, 2002) and "Wicked Divas, Musical Theater, and Internet Girl Fans" (*Camera Obscura* 65, 22.2 [2007]: 39–71).

8. In stressing the dynamic of performance and (re)creation in musicals, I am both indebted to Bruce Kirle's *Unfinished Show Business: Broadway Musicals as Works-in-Process* (Carbondale: Southern Illinois University Press, 2005) and insistent that the idea of performance be applied as broadly as possible. For related arguments, see Marvin Carlson, *The Haunted Stage: The Theatre as Memory Machine* (Ann Arbor: University of Michigan Press, 2003).

9. For an extended discussion of this aspect of tonality, see Susan McClary, *Conventional Wisdom: The Content of Musical Form* (Berkeley: University of California Press, 2000).

10. Among many accounts of the mismatch among *Candide*'s constituent parts, Stephen Sondheim's is especially memorable: "The book didn't belong with the score, the score didn't belong with the direction, and the direction didn't belong with the book. I thought Lillian [Hellman]'s book was wonderful, but it's very black. The score [by Leonard Bernstein] is pastiche, with bubble and sparkle and sweetness. The direction [by Tyrone Guthrie] was wedding cake, like an operetta" (quoted in *Meryle Secrest's Stephen Sondheim: A Life* [New York: Alfred A. Knopf, 1998], p. 120). For related accounts, see Humphrey Burton, *Leonard Bernstein* (New York: Doubleday, 1994), p. 263 (quoting lyricist Richard Wilbur); Brooks Peters, "Making Your Garden Grow: Lillian Hellman and Candide" (*Opera News* 65.1 [July, 2000]: 38); and Ethan Mordden, *Coming Up Roses; The Broadway Musical in the 1950s* (New York: Oxford University Press, 1998). For accounts of how Harold Prince spearheaded the show's renovation, see chapter 26 of Prince's *Contradictions: Notes on Twenty-Six Years in the Theatre* (New York: Dodd, Mead, 1974); Carol Ilson, *Harold Prince: from Pajama Game to Phantom of*

the Opera (Ann Arbor: UMI Research Press, 1989), pp. 212–25; and Foster Hirsch, *Harold Prince and the American Musical Theatre* (Cambridge: Cambridge University Press, 1989), pp. 149–56.

11. For discussions and examples of what I term the "marriage trope," see my *The American Musical and the Formation of National Identity* (Princeton, NJ: Princeton University Press, 2005) and Knapp, 2006. Rick Altman succinctly describes this aspect of musicals: "The marriage which resolves the primary (sexual) dichotomy also mediates between two terms of the secondary (thematic) opposition" in *The American Film Musical* (Bloomington: Indiana University Press, 1987, p. 50). For revelatory discussions of how this entrenched trope has sometimes transferred to homosocial relationships, often similarly uniting opposites, see Stacy Wolf's "'We'll Always Be Bosom Buddies': Female Duets and the Queering of Broadway Musical Theater" (*GLQ: A Journal of Lesbian and Gay Studies* 12:3 [2006]: 351–76) and "'Defying Gravity': Queer Conventions in the Musical *Wicked*" (*Theatre Journal* 60 [2008]:1–21).

REFERENCES

Selected References for Volume III, Chapter 1

Decker, Todd. "'Big, as in Large, as in Huge': *Dreamgirls* and Difference in the Performance of Gender, Blackness, and Popular Music History." *Twenty-First Century Musicals: From Stage to Screen*. Ed. George Rodosthenous. New York: Routledge, 2018.

———. "'Do You Want to Hear a Mammy Song?': A Historiography of Show *Boat*." *Contemporary Theatre Review* 19.1 (2009): 8–21.

———. *Show Boat: Performing Race in an American Musical*. New York: Oxford University Press, 2013.

———. *Who Should Sing 'Ol' Man River': The Lives of an American Song*. New York: Oxford University Press, 2015.

Dyer, Richard. *In the Space of a Song: The Uses of Song in Film*. New York: Routledge, 2012.

Goldmark, Daniel. "Adapting *The Jazz Singer* from Short Story to Screen: A Musical Profile." *Journal of the American Musicological Society* 70.3 (2017): 767-817.

Hoffman, Warren. *The Great White Way: Race and the Broadway Musical*. New Brunswick, NJ: Rutgers University Press, 2014.

Knapp, Raymond. *The American Musical and the Formation of National Identity*. Princeton, NJ: Princeton University Press, 2005.

Lewis, David H. *Flower Drum Songs: The Story of Two Musicals.* Jefferson, NC: McFarland, 2006.

Mokdad, Linda. "At the Intersection of Music, Sexuality and Race: *Hairspray*'s Generic and Aesthetic Variances." *Twenty-First Century Musicals: From Stage to Screen.* Ed. George Rodosthenous. New York: Routledge, 2018.

Most, Andrea. *Making Americans: Jews and the Broadway Musical.* Cambridge, MA: Harvard University Press, 2004.

Shaw, Lisa. *Carmen Miranda.* London: BFI, 2013.

Tucker, Sophie. *Some of These Days: The Autobiography of Sophie Tucker.* Garden City, NY: Doubleday, Doran and Company, 1945.

Selected References for Volume III, Chapter 2

Carlson, Marvin. *The Haunted Stage: The Theatre as Memory Machine.* Ann Arbor: University of Michigan Press, 2001.

Clum, John M. *Something for the Boys: Musical Theater and Gay Culture.* New York: St. Martin's Press, 1999.

Coleman, Bud and Judith A. Sebesta, eds. *Women In American Musical Theatre: Essays on Composers, Lyricists, Librettists, Arrangers, Choreographers, Designers, Directors, Producers and Performance Artists.* Jefferson, NC: McFarland, 2008.

Doty, Alexander. *Making Things Perfectly Queer: Interpreting Mass Culture.* Minneapolis: University of Minnesota Press, 1993.

Knapp, Raymond. *The American Musical and the Formation of National Identity.* Princeton: Princeton University Press, 2005.

———. *The American Musical and the Performance of National Identity.* Princeton: Princeton University Press, 2006.

Miller, D. A. *Place for Us [Essay on the Broadway Musical].* Cambridge, Massachusetts and London: Harvard University Press, 1998.

Savran, David. *A Queer Sort of Materialism: Recontextualizing American Theater.* Ann Arbor: University of Michigan Press, 2003.

Wolf, Stacy. Changed for Good: A Feminist History of the Broadway Musical. New York: Oxford University Press, 2011.

———. *A Problem Like Maria: Gender and Sexuality in the American Musical.* Ann Arbor: The University of Michigan Press, 2002.

Wollman, Elizabeth. *Hard Times: The Adult Musical in 1970s New York City.* New York: Oxford University Press, 2013.

Selected References for Volume III, Chapter 3

Ayers, Edward L., Patricia Nelson Limerick, Stephen Nissenbaum, and Peter S. Onuf. *All Over the Map: Rethinking American Regions*. Baltimore: Johns Hopkins University Press, 1996.

Campbell, Gavin James. *Music and the Making of a New South*. Chapel Hill: University of North Carolina Press, 2004.

Jones, John Bush. *Our Musicals, Ourselves: A Social History of the American Musical Theatre*. Hanover, NH: Brandeis University Press, 2003.

Kirle, Bruce. *Unfinished Show Business: Broadway Musicals as Works-in-Process*. Carbondale: Southern Illinois University Press, 2005.

Knapp, Raymond. *The American Musical and the Formation of National Identity*. Princeton, NJ: Princeton University Press, 2005.

Most, Andrea. *Making Americans: Jews and the Broadway Musical*. Cambridge, MA: Harvard University Press, 2004.

Savran, David. *A Queer Sort of Materialism: Recontextualizing American Theater*. Ann Arbor: University of Michigan Press, 2003.

Shapiro, Henry D. "How Region Changed Its Meaning and Appalachia Changed Its Standing in the Twentieth Century." *Bridging Southern Cultures: An Interdisciplinary Approach*. Ed. John Lowe. Baton Rouge: Louisiana State University Press, 2005.

Walsh, David and Len Platt. *Musical Theater and American Culture*. Westport, CT: Greenwood, 2003.

Wolf, Stacy. *A Problem Like Maria: Gender and Sexuality in the American Musical*. Ann Arbor: University of Michigan Press, 2002.

Selected References for Volume III, Chapter 4

Adler, Steven. *On Broadway: Art and Commerce on the Great White Way*. Carbondale, IL: Southern Illinois University Press, 2004.

Broadway League and Karen Hauser. *The Demographics of the Broadway Audience, 2007–2008*. New York: Broadway League, 2008.

Butsch, Richard. *The Making of American Audiences: From Stage to Television, 1750–1990*. Cambridge: Cambridge University Press, 2000.

DiMaggio, Paul. "Cultural Boundaries and Structural Change: The Extension of the High Culture Model to Theater, Opera, and the Dance, 1900-1940." Lamont, Michèle and Fournier, Marcel, eds., *Cultivating Differences: Symbolic Boundaries and the Making of Inequality*. Chicago: University of Chicago Press, 1992.

Hohenberg, John. *The Pulitzer Prizes: A History of the Awards in Books, Drama, Music, and Journalism, Based on the Private Files over Six Decades*. New York: Columbia University Press, 1974.

Kammen, Michael G. *American Culture, American Tastes: Social Change and the 20th Century*. New York: Knopf, 1999.

Levine, Lawrence W. *Highbrow/Lowbrow: The Emergence of Cultural Hierarchy in America*. Cambridge, MA: Harvard University Press, 1988.

Nathan, George Jean. *The Popular Theatre*. New York: Knopf, 1918, revised 1923.

Poggi, Jack. *Theater in America: The Impact of Economic Forces, 1870–1967*. Ithaca, NY: Cornell University Press, 1968.

Savran, David. *A Queer Sort of Materialism: Recontextualizing American Theater*. Ann Arbor: University of Michigan Press, 2003.

———. *Highbrow/Lowdown: Theater, Jazz and the Making of the New Middle Class*. Ann Arbor, MI: University of Michigan Press, 2009.

Taylor, Ronald, ed. *Aesthetics and Politics*. London: Verso, 1980.

Toohey, John L. *A History of the Pulitzer Prize Plays*. New York: Citadel Press, 1967.

Selected References for Volume III, Chapter 5

Adler, Steven. *On Broadway: Art and Commerce on the Great White Way*. Carbondale: Southern Illinois University Press, 2004.

Breglio, John. *I Wanna Be a Producer: How to Make a Killing on Broadway . . . or Get Killed*. New York: Applause Books, 2016.

Farber, Donald C. *Producing Theatre: A Comprehensive and Legal Business Guide* (3rd edition). New York: Limelight Books, 2006.

Hirsch, Foster. *The Boys from Syracuse: The Shuberts' Theatrical Empire*. Carbondale: Southern Illinois University Press, 2000.

Kissel, Howard. *David Merrick: The Abominable Showman: The Unauthorized Biography*. New York: Applause Books, 1993.

Prince, Harold. *Sense of Occasion*. New York: Applause Books, 2017.

Riedel, Michael. *Razzle Dazzle: The Battle for Broadway.* New York: Simon and Schuster, 2015.

Selected References for Volume III, Chapter 6

Bennett, Susan. *Theatre Audiences: A Theory of Production and Reception,* 2nd ed. (London: Routledge, 1997).

Butsch, Richard. *The Making of American Audiences: From Stage to Television, 1750–1990* (Cambridge: Cambridge University Press, 2000).

Dolan, Jill, *The Feminist Spectator in Action: Feminist Criticism for the Stage and Screen* (New York: Palgrave Macmillan, 2013).

Show Business: The Road to Broadway, directed by Dori Berinstein, 2007 (Liberation Entertainment DVD release, 2007).

Suskin, Steven. *More Opening Nights on Broadway: A Critical Quotebook of the Musical Theatre, 1965 through 1981* (New York: Schirmer Books, 1997).

Suskin, Steven, *Opening Nights on Broadway: A Critical Quotebook of the Golden Age of the Musical Theatre, Oklahoma! to Fiddler on the Roof* (New York: Schirmer Books, 1990).

Wolf, Stacy. *A Problem Like Maria: Gender and Sexuality in the American Musical* (Ann Arbor: University of Michigan Press, 2002).

Selected References for Volume III, Chapter 7

Duffett, Mark, ed. *Popular Music Fandom: Identities, Roles, and Practices.* New York: Routledge, 2013.

Dyer, Richard. *Heavenly Bodies.* London: Routledge, 2004.

———. *Stars.* London: British Film Institute, 1998.

Gledhill, Christine, ed. *Stardom: Industry of Desire.* London: Routledge, 1991.

Hills, Matt. *Fan Cultures.* London: Routledge, 2002.

Jenkins, Henry. *Textual Poachers: Television Fans and Participatory Culture.* London: Routledge, 1992.

Leonardi, Susan J. and Rebecca A. Pope. *The Diva's Mouth: Body, Voice, Prima Donna Politics.* New Brunswick, NJ: Rutgers University Press, 1996.

Lewis, Lisa A., ed. *The Adoring Audience: Fan Culture and Popular Media*. London: Routledge, 1992.

Stacey, Jackie. *Star Gazing: Hollywood Cinema and Female Spectatorship*. London: Routledge, 1994.

Wolf, Stacy. "Wicked Divas, Musical Theater, and Internet Girl Fans." *Camera Obscura* 65 22.2 (2007): 39–71.

Selected References for Volume III, Chapter 8

Bennett, Jeff. *Secondary Stages: Revitalizing High School Theatre*. Portsmouth, NH: Heinemann, 2001.

Chansky, Dorothy. *Composing Ourselves: The Little Theatre Movement and the American Audience*. Carbondale: Southern Illinois University Press, 2004.

Chapman, Jennifer. "Heteronormativity and High School Theatre." Ph.D. dissertation, University of Wisconsin-Madison, 2005.

Cohen, Leah Hager. *The Stuff of Dreams: Behind the Scenes of an American Community Theatre*. New York: Viking Penguin, 2001.

Gard, Robert E., and Gertrude Burley. *Community Theatre: Idea and Achievement*. New York: Duell, Sloan, and Pearce, 1959.

Gonzalez, Jo Beth. *Temporary Stages: Departing from Tradition in High School Theatre Education*. Portsmouth, NH: Heinemann, 2006.

Harbin, Shirley, Jennifer Roberts, Noelia Saenz, and Carl P. Grant, eds. *Millennium Theatres: Discovering Community Theatre's Future by Exploring Its Past*. Detroit: Theatre USA, the American Association of Community Theatre, and the City of Detroit Department of Recreation, Empowerment Zone, 2004.

Hume, Samuel J. and Lois M. Foster. *Theatre and School*. New York: Samuel French, 1932

Macgowan, Kenneth. *The Theatre of Tomorrow*. New York: Boni and Liveright, 1921.

van de Water, Manon and Annie Giannini. "Gay and Lesbian Theatre for Young People, or the Representation of 'Troubled Youth.'" *We Will Be Citizens: New Essays on Gay and Lesbian Theatre*. Ed. James Fisher. Jefferson, NC: McFarland, 2008, pp. 103–22.

Selected References for Volume III, Chapter 9

Knapp, Raymond. *The American Musical and the Performance of Personal Identity*. Princeton, NJ: Princeton University Press, 2006.

———. *Making Light: Haydn, Musical Camp, and the Long Shadow of Musical Idealism*. Durham: Duke University Press, 2018.

Morris, Mitchell. *The Persistence of Sentiment: Essays on Pop Music in the '70s*. Berkeley and Los Angeles: University of California Press, 2012.

Savran, David. *Highbrow/Lowdown: Theater, Jazz, and the Making of the New Middle Class*. Ann Arbor: University of Michigan Press, 2009.

———. *A Queer Sort of Materialism: Recontextualizing American Theater*. Ann Arbor: University of Michigan Press, 2003.

Stilwell, Robynn. "Music of the Youth Revolution: Rock through the 1960s." *The Cambridge History of Twentieth-Century Music*. Ed. Nicholas Cook and Anthony Pople. Cambridge: Cambridge University Press, 2004, pp. 418–52.

Wald, Elijah. *How the Beatles Destroyed Rock 'n' Roll: An Alternative History of American Popular Music*. New York: Oxford University Press, 2009.

Wollman, Elizabeth. *The Theater Will Rock: A History of the Rock Musical from Hair to Hedwig*. Ann Arbor: University of Michigan Press, 2006.

INDEX

Note: Page numbers in *italics* indicate photographs.